OLD TESTAMENT CHALLENGE

IMPLEMENTATION GUIDE

OLD TESTAMENT CHALLENGE

IMPLEMENTATION GUIDE

KEVIN HARNEY
MINDY CALIGUIRE

GRAND RAPIDS, MICHIGAN 49530 USA

We want to hear from you. Please send your comments about this book to us in care of zreview@zondervan.com. Thank you.

ZONDERVAN™

Old Testament Challenge Implementation Guide

Requests for information should be addressed to:

Zondervan, *Grand Rapids, Michigan 49530*

ISBN 0-310-24939-2

Interior design by Sharon VanLoozenoord

Interior composition by Beth Shagene

Printed in the United States of America

03 04 05 06 07 08 09 /❖ VG/ 10 9 8 7 6 5 4 3 2 1

CONTENTS

FOREWORD

I want to tell you why I'm so passionate about the Old Testament Challenge and why I think it has the potential to change the lives of individuals and whole churches. There are several reasons I'll mention, but the most important one can be summed up in a single word.

Jesus.

From a human perspective, the Hebrew Scriptures were the single most important factor in shaping the way Jesus thought about his Father. In our day people will occasionally talk as if there is some discrepancy between the God Jesus taught about and the God of the Old Testament. Such a discrepancy would have been unthinkable to Jesus himself. The Scriptures fed his mind and soul the way physical nourishment fed his body. There is simply no way to have the mind of Christ formed in us—to think and perceive and feel and believe the way he did—without having our minds shaped by the same words that shaped his.

Part of what I love about the Old Testament Challenge is that it allows people to go through the Scriptures in community. On our own, we have a hard time keeping up a commitment to jog regularly, let alone pursue a spiritual discipline that our fallenness will resist tenaciously. But by combining an individualized reading plan with small-group study *and* a large-group teaching component, people can achieve together what they never could in isolation.

This brings me to another benefit of the Old Testament Challenge. At our church (Willow Creek Community Church), we often found that people suffered from "spiritual information overload." They would hear one talk at a weekend service and another during our mid-week worship time; they would discuss a third topic in their small group and look at a fourth one in their personal reading. It was like drinking from a fire hydrant. Integrating the input people were receiving in their spiritual lives had a revolutionary impact on their spiritual growth.

It also meant that people could *finally* feel as if they were making some progress on one of the great challenges facing the church in our day: biblical literacy. Many people are prevented from gaining much nourishment from the Bible because they lack a big picture perspective of what is going on. They don't know the overarching story. This is not the sort of thing that can be gained overnight. It is possible to do great seminars on topics like relational skills or financial management, but biblical literacy cannot be microwaved.

Finally, I'm excited about the Old Testament Challenge because it doesn't simply help people gain information about the Hebrew Scriptures; it encourages people to meet God there. The purpose of the writers of the Scriptures was never simply to fill minds but always to renew them: to soften hearts and strengthen knees and challenge spirits. The material you are about to go through serves as a kind of bridge between the mysterious world of ancient Israel and the world in which we work, navigate friendships, pay our bills, and do our living and dying. It helps us bring all our lives under the authority and guidance of this book that shaped our Lord.

The Old Testament has lost none of its power. All that remains is for you to take the Challenge. I hope you do.

—John Ortberg

ACKNOWLEDGMENTS

Before this was ever a published resource, the Old Testament Challenge (OTC) was birthed out of a living experience deeply rooted in the life of the local church. The OTC as a product is the culmination of great efforts by two churches—Willow Creek Community Church in Illinois and Corinth Reformed Church in Michigan. These acknowledgments are offered on behalf of all OTC components in gratitude to those who were part of the OTC experiences at both churches. Because of the OTC's integrated and comprehensive approach (involving main services, small groups, and individuals), we could not have completed this project without the dedication and work of many people. Though space limitations prohibit naming all of them, they include the following:

- Creig Day, who served as project manager throughout Willow's pre-launch and launch phases and provided day-to-day collaborative leadership to the core team.
- Willow Creek's programming leadership and video teams, who produced and executed OTC creative elements, especially Doug Veenstra, Pam Howell, Sherri Meyer, and Jarrett Stevens.
- Willow Creek staff and volunteers who created, edited, printed, and distributed the weekly small-group curriculum, individual reading guides, and the promotional pieces used to launch and maintain momentum for the Old Testament Challenge. These include Rob Stevens, Dennis and Cynthia Lubecke, Carla Howe, Jill Williams, Lisa Gilliana, Sally Shoemaker, Kim Savage, Anne Frost, and Chris Braniff.
- Willow Creek volunteers who contributed to the creation of the individual reading plan, including Kelly Boyd, and Jill and Rob Williams.
- The Willow Creek website team, including Mort Mease, Rachael Singh, Camile Burner, Keith Baldwin, Larry Butterfield, and Pat Friedline. This dedicated team developed and maintained a variety of creative games, quizzes, and downloadable curriculum resources to support the OTC experience online.
- Tiffany Staman, assistant to John Ortberg; and Kate Maver, whose research expertise was an enormous help in crafting OTC messages.
- Bill Hybels, senior pastor of Willow Creek Community Church. Bill loved the idea of challenging the New Community to such a bold commitment. He strongly supported the Old Testament Challenge and provided ongoing encouragement to those directly involved.

- Small-group leaders at both churches who not only took the challenge personally but who also led groups through the OTC. These leaders helped individuals apply biblical truths in their daily lives. Way to go!
- Warren Burgess, Ryan Pazdur, and Don Porter, teaching pastors at Corinth Reformed Church, who partnered with Kevin Harney in preaching OTC messages and brought their love of God's Word and their own unique insights to this project.
- Ryan Pazdur, for creativity and assistance in developing OTC PowerPoint® resources.
- Don Porter, who developed the Frequently Asked Questions (FAQ) resources for all forty weeks and did an excellent job of crafting solid answers to a host of tough questions.
- The congregations of Willow Creek Community Church and Corinth Reformed Church, both of whom took the challenge and immersed themselves in the Old Testament for the better part of a year. We are grateful for your commitment and your hunger for God's Word. It was a joy to open the Bible and study it each week with communities who so passionately desired to know and follow God better.
- Willow Creek Association staff, led by Jim Mellado, and especially the publishing and marketing teams under the leadership of Joe Sherman. During the year we experienced and developed OTC as a publishable resource, these individuals provided practical help and encouragement and kept before us the value of OTC to other churches. We are particularly grateful for the expertise and support of Charlene Perez, Nancy Raney, Christine M. Anderson, and Doug Yonamine.
- The Zondervan publishing team, who did an amazing job of keeping a mammoth project moving forward. Jack Kuhatschek's insights were instrumental in helping to create the OTC concept; John Raymond quarterbacked the publishing process from beginning to end; T.J. Rathbun managed postproduction for all video segments; Jean Bloom kept all schedules on track; Alicia Mey strategized the most effective ways to bring OTC to local churches; and Verlyn Verbrugge brought the mind of a scholar and heart of a pastor to editing hundreds of manuscript pages. If ever there were an Olympic event for publishing, you would be our dream team!

—John Ortberg, Judson Poling, Mindy Caliguire, Kevin Harney, Sherry Harney

Preface

This *Implementation Guide* provides a comprehensive tour through the Old Testament Challenge experience. It is an A-to-Z overview of the full experience, giving you, the OTC leader, all the tools you need to rally church support, build a leadership team, prepare for the Old Testament Challenge, launch the OTC, lead the thirty-two-week[1] experience and end the Old Testament Challenge in a way that propels your church forward with a new passion and commitment to God's Word. Because this is such a comprehensive, church-wide experience, it is critical that your leadership team work together to integrate the Old Testament Challenge into the life of the congregation for maximum impact.

The vision of the Old Testament Challenge is to help a church engage those who attend in a comprehensive experience of God's Word that touches on three distinct levels simultaneously: to bring people through a learning experience of the Old Testament as a *congregation*, in *small groups*, and in *individual study* of the Bible.

To understand why the three-level, integrated approach is so important, imagine a woman in a local church who is a deeply committed follower of Jesus. She is attending worship each week as the pastor preaches a message series entitled *Life Lessons from the Sermon on the Mount*. She is learning and growing as the whole congregation studies the great truths of Matthew 5–7. She is also part of a small group that is doing a study on the book of Psalms. Again, she is learning and growing, but the content from her small group and congregational teaching don't really connect. Along with these learning times, each morning she spends time reading the book of Romans in her personal study of the Bible.

All three of the woman's learning experiences are rich. Each one offers new insights into the Bible and impacts her life. But there are times she feels somewhat overwhelmed. She has three streams of learning, they are all biblical, but it just feels like a lot to take in and apply on a daily basis.

Now imagine the same woman another way. She comes to church and hears a dynamic message on the opening chapters of Genesis that focuses on God's dream for community with the people he has created. It touches her heart and brings practical challenges to her life. The next morning she wakes up and begins her morning study in the book of Genesis. As she reads, she is prompted to reflect and

[1]The Old Testament Challenge includes thirty-two weeks of congregational messages and small group studies. For individuals, the OTC offers two options for reading through the Old Testament—a thirty-two-week plan and a forty-week plan. The thirty-two-week option is a "fast-track" reading plan that directly parallels weekly OTC messages. Those following this plan read only key Old Testament passages. The forty-week reading plan enables participants to read the entire Old Testament—every word! It requires an additional eight weeks beyond the thirty-two-week OTC experience to complete.

dig deeper through a daily reading guide that helps her walk through the portion of the Bible that she heard preached that week. Later that week, she meets with her small group, and they open Genesis and look even more deeply at what it means to be in community with God and each other.

These three different learning experiences all grow out of the same portion of Scripture and reinforce each other. The next week the message in church, her small group, and her personal study move the woman into the next part of the Old Testament. Now imagine this happening for thirty-two weeks as she walks through the major passages, life stories, and themes of the entire Old Testament.

If you can see the benefits of this approach, you will begin to get a sense for the power of the Old Testament Challenge. This is not just another study through the Bible. It is a life-changing journey that engages Christ's followers on three critical levels of life and learning. This Old Testament Challenge *Implementation Guide* gives you everything you need to walk your congregation through the OTC on all three levels. From the first phase of mobilizing your leadership to the final phase of celebrating the conclusion of the Old Testament Challenge, and everything in-between, this guide gives you all the tools you need to make it an experience your congregation will never forget.

Introduction to the Old Testament Challenge

CHAPTER 1

DISCOVERING THE POWER OF GOD'S WORD

The Old Testament Challenge has been created to help local churches and followers of Christ *discover the life-changing relevance of God's Word.* Specifically, it has been designed to move a whole congregation deeply into the two-thirds of the Bible that often get overlooked, the Old Testament. Churches that take this challenge enter a process of immersing themselves in God's Word in a way that will change them forever.

Old Testament "Challenge"

Some of the best experiences in life involve a challenge, and this is certainly true when it comes to a comprehensive study of the Old Testament. This OTC experience is a challenge because it involves asking an entire congregation to maintain focus on their study of the Old Testament over a period of thirty-two weeks. In a day when attention spans are getting shorter and shorter, this takes a serious commitment.

It is also a challenge because each person will be invited to participate in a small-group experience that will include transparent sharing, intentional accountability, and life growth in the context of a small community of Christ-followers.

Finally, this is a challenge because each person will have an opportunity to study through the entire Old Testament on a personal level by using the OTC individual reading guide. This will be a first for many, but certainly a life-impacting challenge for all.

The Issue of Biblical Literacy

An honest evaluation of most Christ-followers would yield this simple truth: Many Christians today are illiterate when it comes to the Old Testament. They might dabble in the New Testament or even study it faithfully, but the Old Testament does not get a lot of attention. Sure, the Psalms are read on occasion and some of the classic Old Testament stories are told to children (usually tamed-down versions from children's storybooks), but serious study of the Old Testament is a rare thing these days. It seems as if the culture and context of the Old Testament don't connect easily for many modern readers. On top of this, many followers of Christ struggle because they feel that some of the teaching of the Old Testament conflicts with the New Testament. Whatever the reasons, Christ-followers today often avoid the Old Testament.

For the most part, churches aren't doing much better than individuals in this regard. Many churches spend limited time preaching from the Old Testament in weekly services. Systematic and intentional study of the entire Old Testament is on the endangered species list when it comes to what kind of commitments churches are making these days. The sad truth is that pastors (who wholeheartedly believe the Old Testament is God's inspired Word) spend little time expounding it.

Philip Yancey, in his book *The Bible Jesus Read*, looks at the reality of Old Testament illiteracy. He writes:

> A Wheaton College professor named Gary Burge has found that ignorance of the Old Testament extends to the church as well. For several years Burge has been testing incoming freshmen at his school, a premier evangelical institution. His survey shows that students who have attended Sunday school all their lives, have watched innumerable episodes of *Veggie Tales*, and who have listened to countless sermons, cannot identify basic facts about the Old Testament.

With this reality in mind, the leadership team of Willow Creek Community Church realized that many of those who attended needed to grow in their knowledge of the Bible in general, and of the Old Testament specifically.

The Willow Creek Story

The OTC concept began as a brainstorming idea at a Willow Creek senior leadership meeting. On the principle that there are no bad ideas at a brainstorming session, the Old Testament Challenge began as one of those outrageous concepts that got floated in the discussion, but everyone knew there was a good chance it would end up as just scribbles on another flip-chart page destined for the circular file.

But the more we talked about it, the more we began to wonder: What if we really did it? What if everyone actually read the entire Old Testament as our teaching pastor, John Ortberg, taught through it? What if small groups studied and discussed each message and took the biblical learning to an even deeper level?

At a planning session for future message topics, the leadership team decided to go for it. For an entire ministry year, we would immerse the congregation in the Old Testament, daring ourselves and the congregation to a large-scale Old Testament Challenge!

We challenged each attendee to an aggressive reading plan for getting through the entire Old Testament. At the same time, John Ortberg taught through the Old Testament during mid-week worship services. Many creative elements were used to add humor and bring clarity to often-confusing topics, such as animal sacrifices, dietary laws, holy wars, polygamy, and other difficulties that arise when studying the Old Testament. Small groups were strongly encouraged to participate by using a new curriculum developed and written for the OTC. The goal was for groups to discuss, in depth, the ideas presented during each week's service.

Throughout the year we received a flood of notes, phone calls, and e-mail messages expressing deep gratitude for how OTC was helping people grow spiritually and helping them to understand concepts that had previously been difficult to grasp. Small-group participants expressed appreciation for the opportunity to process what they had learned in congregational gatherings with their small-group members on a more personal level. Out of this experience emerged a strong sense of what we were learning together as a church. Our sense of community grew stronger. We felt we were on an important journey together as we dug deep into the Old Testament and watched as God formed our hearts with the Word.

Thousands of people from Willow Creek Community Church walked with us through this experience of learning and growth. We began in Genesis and heard God speak the heavens and earth into existence. We ended several months later as the people of Israel were set free from captivity in Babylon and were allowed to return to the Promised Land, filled with hope and joy. Along the way, we learned lessons about God, faith, and ourselves that will continue to impact us for a lifetime.

The Corinth Story

When we were just a few weeks into the Old Testament Challenge, we wondered if our experience could be transferred to another community of Christ-followers. Could OTC work at other churches? We decided to partner with another church to find out. What we learned was both encouraging and exciting!

Corinth Reformed Church in Grand Rapids, Michigan, is much smaller than Willow Creek. We thought it would be a great opportunity to discover whether the OTC could be successfully adapted to a very different setting. The Willow team gave the staff at Corinth all the resources that were being developed for the OTC. The leaders at Corinth took these resources and built on them. The goal was not to duplicate the exact same experience as Willow was having, but to create a unique learning experience for themselves as they walked through the Old Testament Challenge.

The experiment paid off! The attenders at Corinth shared the same passion and excitement for the Old Testament as did those at Willow. The whole church studied through the thirty-two messages as a congregation, many studied the small-group materials, and individuals also committed to read through the entire Old Testament on their own in forty weeks,[2] using the weekly study tools developed at Willow.

[2]The Old Testament Challenge includes thirty-two weeks of congregational messages and small group studies. For individuals, the OTC offers two options for reading through the Old Testament—a thirty-two-week plan and a forty-week plan. The thirty-two-week option is a "fast-track" reading plan that directly parallels weekly OTC messages. Those following this plan read only key Old Testament passages. The forty-week reading plan enables participants to read the entire Old Testament—every word! It requires an additional eight weeks beyond the thirty-two-week OTC experience to complete.

A Larger Vision

When it became clear that these resources would work in other churches as effectively as they had at Willow Creek, we caught an even larger vision for OTC. We began to see that this church-wide experience might be used by other congregations across the nation and around the world.

Imagine what could happen in your church if the entire congregation were to take this Old Testament Challenge. You launch into an extended journey of learning that touches the life of every person who takes the challenge. Biblical knowledge is lifted to a whole new level. People develop a discipline of regular study of Scripture that could stay with them for the rest of their lives. Small groups go deep into the Word and build lines of accountability and encouragement that vaults followers of Christ to new places of commitment and spiritual growth. Moreover, your whole congregation gains a sense of God's pleasure and joy as you grow to know and love him more. It can happen.

Willow Creek and Corinth Reformed Church both took the challenge and discovered that this kind of sustained focus on biblical teaching and study propelled an entire *congregation*, *small groups,* and *individuals* forward toward God's plan for his people and church. This focus on solid biblical teaching on all three levels strengthened these churches, and it will do the same for any local church that takes this challenge and dives deep into God's Word.

Congregation. The teaching for a full thirty-two sessions covers relevant topics in the Old Testament, providing a firm foundational understanding of the Hebrew Scriptures and teachings leading up to the life and ministry of Jesus.

Small groups.[3] The wisdom of topics such as Proverbs is discussed in depth, and group members are personally supported in their efforts to grow spiritually.

Individuals. The reading guide enables individuals to read the assigned text and interact with questions and related New Testament passages.

Value of an Old Testament Challenge

For someone who is attending the congregational services, involved in a small group, and also reading through the Scriptures on his or her own, the Old Testament Challenge becomes an ideal environment for authentic spiritual growth. Here are several benefits you can expect when you take the OTC.

Time. The OTC provides adequate time for people to "process" these truths, making personal application to their own lives. Nearly an entire year devoted to understanding the message of the Old Testament allows ample time for absorption and real learning.

[3]Note that what the *Implementation Guide* refers to as "small groups" is a gathering of people that could take place in adult Sunday school classes, cell groups, or some other format. To keep references clear, we refer to all such formats as "small groups," with the understanding that the dynamics of a small group can find expression in a variety of ways.

Simplicity. The Old Testament Challenge also has a strong simplicity factor. Oftentimes, people bounce around thematically between a great teaching message, whatever their small group happens to be studying at the time, and any personal study they do. The OTC brings focus to the topic of study for a year, simplifying the process of authentic spiritual growth.

Community. The Old Testament Challenge enables you to experience spiritual growth in community. Rarely does a congregation seek to make progress on so many levels *together*. When we meet each week at the large-group gathering, we all know the issues we have been reading about and discussing since we last met. We develop a common language, a common focus. We are seeking to grow as companions. This is a rare experience in a church, and deeply powerful.

Biblical literacy. An increase in biblical literacy means that a greater number of people in the congregation understand the basic doctrines of the Christian faith. They understand and experience more of the true nature of God; they connect ideas and images from the Old Testament with learning in the New Testament.

Teaching resource. The OTC teaching resource provides a training tool for teachers as they interact with sound biblical teaching and effective communication strategies.

Spiritual formation. The central task, ultimately, of the local church, is to contribute to the lifelong process of people being formed into the image of Christ. The integrated approach of the Old Testament Challenge provides an optimal environment for the sometimes elusive process of spiritual formation to actually take root in a local congregation.

Reaching the goal. And, of course, at the end of The Old Testament Challenge, it's so great to look back and know what you've accomplished as a community. At the end of this year, together you can say, "We've accomplished an incredible goal—and we've done it together!"

The resource you hold in your hands is the realization of a dream. We believe it came from the heart of God, was birthed at Willow Creek, and has been tested and proven effective in the local church. A team of writers, editors, pastors, and leaders has worked together to refine all of these resources and make them accessible for use in virtually any congregation. Our hope is that you will now be able to walk with your congregation through the adventure of the Old Testament Challenge. As God speaks and moves through this experience, we believe your church will never be the same.

Old Testament Challenge Components

CHAPTER 2

To help you get a picture of all the resources in the OTC kit, here is a brief overview of every OTC component that has been developed to help you walk through the Old Testament Challenge.

Teaching Guide

Each OTC kit has a guide designed to help the teacher craft messages tailored to his or her audience. There are many different elements in the Teacher's Resource Guide:

- ***Creative Message Idea:*** Offers a broad variety of ideas a teacher can use to bring home a biblical point with power. This section includes video segments developed specifically for the OTC messages as well as ideas for using props or other visual aids.
- ***Heart of the Message:*** A brief description of the central theme of the entire message.
- ***Heart of the Messenger:*** Provides direction for how the teacher can prepare to study and open his or her heart to what the Holy Spirit wants to say.
- ***Historical Context Note:*** A number of texts make much more sense when we have an understanding of Old Testament culture. These notes provide this kind of background information.
- ***Illustration:*** Ideas for illustrating core Old Testament concepts.
- ***Interpretive Insight:*** Solid biblical interpretation that functions as the backbone of the message.
- ***Life Application:*** Practical suggestions for life application. Sometimes these ideas are specific, giving detailed instruction on concrete ways a congregation can respond to God's Word. At other times they are more general, intended to encourage individual reflection on specific application options.
- ***Narrative on Life:*** Examples of powerful life stories. These can be used as printed in the teacher's guide or retold in the teacher's own words.
- ***Narrative on the Text:*** Retells the biblical story. Some sections of John Ortberg's original messages are in a form that can be read as is by the

teacher. They can also become a source of ideas as the teacher tells the story in a narrative form that fits his or her own communication style.

- ***New Testament Connection:*** Points out the natural connections between the Old and New Testaments.
- ***On the Lighter Side:*** Provides two kinds of humorous insights: biblical passages or insights that have a humorous aspect to them; and ideas for stories or jokes that hit a main theme in the message.
- ***Pause for Prayer:*** Suggestions for moments a teacher might want to move naturally into prayer right in the middle of a message.
- ***Pause for Reflection:*** Ideas for when a teacher might want to pause for silence in the middle of the message. These moments can be used to listen, process the lessons learned, and reflect on personal life-application goals.
- ***Significant Scripture:*** A list of significant Scriptures for that portion of the message.
- ***Quotable Quote:*** Great quotes related to the main points of the message from Christians throughout the ages.
- ***Word Study:*** Background explanations of words in the Bible designed to help a passage come alive and make sense.

CDs of the OTC Messages

Each kit includes a set of audio CDs with all of the original Old Testament Challenge messages as they were taught at Willow Creek Community Church.

Video Resource

Every OTC kit contains a video cassette and a DVD with four creative video segments. Some of these are general topics that can be used anywhere in the seven to nine weeks during which that kit is being used. Others are specific to a certain message. When a video segment is designed for a specific message, this is indicated in the Teacher's Resource Guide.

Small-Group Study

Each OTC kit includes one copy of the OTC Small-Group Discussion Guide. Additional copies can be purchased for all those who want to be part of an OTC small group. These studies provide seven to nine sessions that follow the teaching schedule of the Old Testament Challenge. Each session has Scripture readings, small-group questions, and written pieces to spark meaningful and deep discussion. At the end of each study booklet is a collection of leader's notes to help both participants and leaders as they prepare for their small-group gathering.

These small-group studies also include occasional word studies and quotes to help participants go deeper into the topic of the study.

Individual Reading Resource

One of the primary goals of the Old Testament Challenge is to help followers of Christ see the life-changing relevance of God's Word. The best way to do this is to help them dig into the Bible on a regular basis. In an effort to accomplish this, Judson Poling has laid out the entire Old Testament in forty weeks of reading, entitled *Taking the Old Testament Challenge: A Daily Reading Guide*. Individuals who decide to read the entire Old Testament will have a tool to walk them through it. For those who feel they cannot commit to the entire forty weeks, a "short-track" thirty-two-week study guide is also included, with each week's lesson corresponding to material in the small-group discussion guide and the teacher guide. One reading resource is provided in the OTC kit; additional copies can be purchased for those who commit to do the OTC reading.

CD-ROM (Frequently Asked Questions and PowerPoint®)

Another valuable resource provided in the Old Testament Challenge resource kit is a CD-ROM. This CD has two items that can be used as your congregation walks through the OTC:

1. Each OTC kit contains ten, two-page documents that answer frequently asked questions (FAQs) about the Old Testament. There is one FAQ document for each week of the OTC Individual Reading Guide. FAQs can be uploaded to your website and accessed electronically, or printed and distributed each week before or after the service.
2. Each OTC kit contains PowerPoint® presentations for every message in that kit.
3. Each OTC kit contains an interactive game, "Are You an Old Testament Expert?" with several units. These can be used in a worship service or a teaching setting, they can be put on your churches web site, or you may find some other creative way to use it.

As you look at all the resources provided in the OTC kit, you may think you have more than you need for each week. This is intentional. Our goal is to provide a wealth of resources and then let you prayerfully decide what best fits your setting. We also trust the Holy Spirit to guide your preparation process and give you new ideas that work in your unique ministry context. Our prayer is that God will richly bless you as you open his Word and faithfully bring it to his people!

Overview of the Old Testament Challenge's Six Phases

CHAPTER 3

Implementing the Old Testament Challenge is accomplished in six phases.

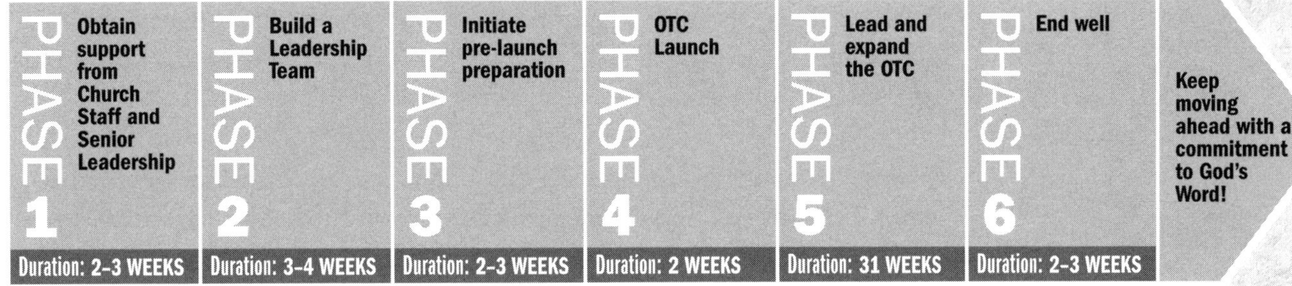

PHASE 1 | Obtain Support from Church Staff and Senior Church Leaders (2–3 Weeks)

The purpose of phase 1 is to obtain support for doing the Old Testament Challenge from church staff and senior church leaders and to draft a preliminary implementation plan.

PHASE 2 | Build a Leadership Team (3–4 Weeks)

The purpose of this phase is to recruit, inspire, and equip the leaders who will launch and maintain a strong Old Testament Challenge experience on all three levels—congregational, small group, and individual study.

PHASE 3 | Initiate Pre-Launch Preparation (2–3 Weeks)

The purpose of phase 3 is to do all the preparation work for launching the Old Testament Challenge. This includes casting vision in the congregation, promoting the Old Testament Challenge, and calling the entire congregation to seriously consider what level of commitment they will make to the OTC .

PHASE 4 | OTC Launch (2 Weeks)

Phase 4 launches all three levels of the OTC (congregation, small groups, and individual study) with excitement and momentum.

PHASE 5 | Lead and Expand the Old Testament Challenge (31 Weeks)

The purpose of phase 5 is to keep the momentum of the OTC going strong through solid leadership, which expands the impact of each resource on the church.

PHASE 6 | End Well (2–3 Weeks)

This final phase provides a strong sense of closure and accomplishment by celebrating all that God has done and by evaluating the effectiveness of the OTC experience at every level.

The description of each phase in the following chapters includes all needed steps for guiding you through the necessary decisions to be made, meetings to convene, leadership to put in place, planning to be done, and all other details for each phase to be successfully completed. Many phases contain sample documents that can be adapted for use in your setting and specific ideas for you to consider as you implement the OTC in your church.

The timeline above gives an estimated duration for each phase and provides a visual representation of the phases so you can see the levels of effort involved over the course of the entire experience. Note the tremendous effort involved in the first three phases; the most arduous work is the successful vision-casting and launch.

A checklist of the entire process, noting every step of each phase, appears on page 60 in the appendix and can be used to track progress as you move through the implementation of the Old Testament Challenge.

Now, you're ready to move into phase 1, where you'll begin the process of casting vision and gaining support from your church staff and senior leadership.

Bon voyage!

CHAPTER

PHASE 1 | Obtain Support from Church Staff and Senior Church Leaders

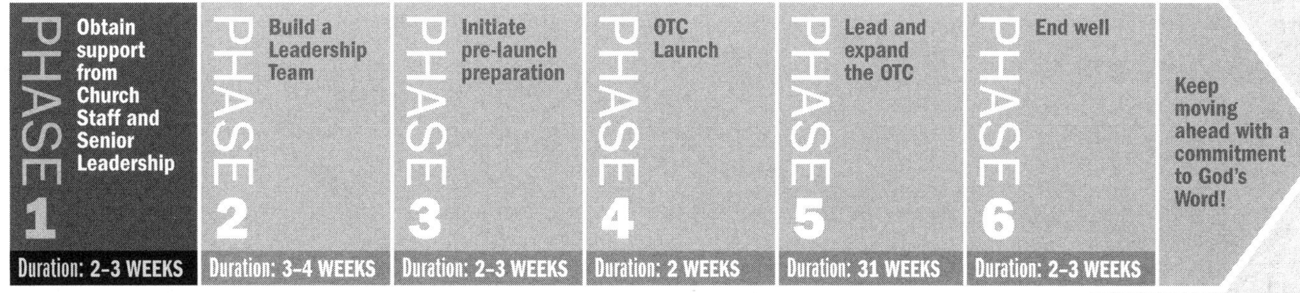

Overview

PURPOSE

The purpose of this phase is to obtain the support from church staff and senior church leaders for doing the Old Testament Challenge and to draft a preliminary implementation plan.

STEPS

The steps involved with obtaining support and developing the plan are these:

Step 1: Present the Old Testament Challenge vision to church staff and secure their support.

Step 2: Present the Old Testament Challenge vision to senior church leaders and secure their support.

Step 3: Create a preliminary implementation plan and timeline.

IMPORTANCE

Effectively launching and maintaining momentum for the OTC requires strong commitment from both staff and senior church leaders. To secure their support and approval, it is vitally important to cast a compelling vision for the impact and benefits of the OTC and to develop a preliminary implementation plan to guide you through the process of bringing the OTC experience to your congregation.

CAUTIONS

Because the OTC is such a comprehensive experience, it is important to consider the impact it will have on every area of your church. This includes everything from ministries such as Sunday school and worship services to website support and the volume of calls that could inundate your receptionist. As you draft your preliminary implementation plan, make every effort to anticipate both the challenges and opportunities of launching the OTC and how you will respond.

Step 1: Present the Old Testament Challenge Vision to Church Staff and Secure Their Support

Why start with staff?

There is no way to do the OTC without the support of your staff.[4] The integrated approach requires the full support of and even new levels of cooperation between many areas of ministry that typically work independently of one another. Additionally, when you approach the senior leadership of the church with the OTC vision, it is important to have already secured the support of those who will carry it out, particularly those involved in planning services, teaching, and providing leadership to small groups.

Whose support is needed, and why?

Key staff leaders will be involved in implementing the OTC throughout the planning and execution of the experience. Those involved in planning weekly services and those who influence small groups need to be especially enthusiastic about the value of the OTC and committed to its success. Cast vision to these staff members first.

Below are some staff roles to be considered when gaining support:

- senior pastor
- teaching pastor(s)
- music director or program director
- director of small groups
- director of adult education/spiritual formation
- administrators
- communications director

If these positions are filled by volunteers (unpaid staff), it is just as important to share the vision with them and make sure you are all in this together.

[4]This *Implementation Guide* uses terms such as "senior staff" and assumes your church has a team of paid staff who will collaborate on making the OTC work. If your church does not have enough paid staff to effectively manage the OTC experience, you will need to identify and recruit volunteers who can fill these roles and can function as unpaid staff members. It is vitally important to secure support for the OTC vision from both paid and unpaid staff.

What level of commitment are you looking for from these people?

The Old Testament Challenge requires full commitments from those who plan and execute weekly services, as this is the main venue for teaching. Everything else hinges on the congregational services being devoted to the thirty-two weeks of the OTC. Thus, teachers, music directors, and technical teams will all be directly involved. Their full support is essential to the success of the challenge.

Additionally, you will want to secure the strong support of the small-groups director in order for the OTC to have the maximum impact on your church. While it is unlikely that every small group will participate, the small-groups director will be the one to challenge small groups to join the Old Testament Challenge.

Administrators will be involved in securing resources for those who need them, such as helping to obtain the next OTC teacher's kit or making the small-group curriculum and individual reading guides available to the congregation. With increased inquiries coming into the church, the OTC may require additional work for those who serve the church in support roles such as a receptionist or webmaster.

What's the best way to present the OTC vision to these staff members?

It's generally best to discuss the vision in person, either individually or in a meeting called specifically for this purpose. During this meeting, you should plan to do the following:

- Share your personal passion and vision.
- Present why you think the congregation would benefit from the OTC experience.
- Cast vision for the potential impact of the integrated experience in each of these areas: congregational, small group, and individual.
- Ask for their input and impressions.
- Ask for their full support. If they need to gather more information or are not ready to make this commitment, invite them to pray about it and schedule a meeting to discuss it again when they are ready to make a decision about their commitment to the OTC.

How do you know you're ready for step 2?

When your key staff agrees that the Old Testament Challenge is the right next step for your ministry, then you are ready to take this idea to whatever boards or senior church leaders that will need to give support in order to provide the necessary human and financial resources.

Step 2: Present the Old Testament Challenge Vision to Senior Church Leaders and Secure Their Support

Whose support is needed ?

Determine which boards, committees, and ministry teams will be involved in a decision involving thirty-two weeks of your church's weekly services as well as the commitment of financial and human resources needed to carry out the OTC experience. Boards that provide spiritual and financial oversight should be considered.

Some possibilities include:

- deacon board
- church board
- board of directors
- elder board

What level of commitment is needed?

Your primary goal in this step is to secure approval to launch. This includes the commitment of resources necessary to launch and expand the OTC throughout its duration. Therefore, you will need to come into these meetings with great clarity on what financial and personnel resources are needed.

Financial. What kind of financial commitment needs to be made for the OTC to succeed? In order to know this, you will need to work through the financial worksheets provided on pages 61–62 in the appendix.

Personnel. There will be a significant commitment of staff and volunteer resources for effective implementation of the Old Testament Challenge. It is vitally important to have a number of staff or volunteers in specific roles that will help the OTC run smoothly.

- You need a cross-functional leader—likely the OTC champion—who will integrate the efforts of teachers, music directors, small-group directors, church communications directors, and others to provide a seamless experience for the church. This role is described in greater detail on page 65.
- Also, you may choose to assign someone to lead a communications strategy that will keep the congregation motivated and informed through printed materials and a church website during the OTC.

- The Old Testament Challenge will add to the workload of existing support staff as well. The receptionist may experience an increased call volume. Even the children's ministry could be impacted by increased church attendance.

During phase 1 of the implementation you need to gain approval for devoting staff time for this kind of work. You want the full agreement of any governing boards at the beginning in order to provide the support needed during the OTC.

What preparation is needed to present this vision?

Prepare the financial worksheet (see page 61 of the appendix) in advance.

Ask for sufficient time on the next board meeting agenda. This is not a quick conversation, so be sure to allow enough time to present the complete vision, have discussion, and rally support for the whole OTC experience.

Have your key points ready for the meeting.

It is essential to have a concise and compelling explanation of the rationale behind the OTC and clear descriptions of exactly what you want from these boards and leaders in order to move forward. A sample OTC Vision Overview sheet is in the appendix on page 63. This resource must be adapted for your unique situation but it does provide examples of key points for your presentation.

In many cases, your personal passion for the OTC will be what most strongly impacts your church's leadership. Be sure to emphasize the value of both biblical literacy and spiritual formation through this uniquely integrated approach to church-wide learning.

Lastly, if you move into these meetings with the strong support of staff members who are most directly involved in implementation, it will greatly strengthen your request and demonstrate the level of commitment for this experience that already exists among those who must implement it day to day. Senior leaders will want to know how feasible it is to get so many divergent areas of the church to cooperate. Go in with great support from teammates.

What is the goal of step 2?

By the conclusion of this step, you should have full agreement from senior leaders to proceed with the Old Testament Challenge. This includes their commitment to devote the necessary time, financial resources, and human resources to complete the Challenge. It also includes their personal commitment to give prayer support and to participate enthusiastically in the OTC experience.

Step 3: Create Preliminary Implementation Plan and Timeline

Now that key staff members and senior leaders are ready to take on the Old Testament Challenge, you need to begin assembling your core team. In order to cast vision and recruit those who will be leading, you first need to prepare a preliminary implementation plan and timeline that can become the working plan for the duration of the OTC.

In the preliminary implementation plan, you need to customize all the steps involved in implementing the OTC to the unique needs of your church. Then, use the timeline given to anticipate the amount of time you need to plan, launch, lead, and conclude the OTC.

Take the standard implementation plan presented on page 60 in the appendix and review it to see what changes you need to make for your church. For example, if your church plans to utilize adult Sunday school classes instead of small groups, change the plan to reflect your situation. Go through the entire plan and adapt it so your preliminary implementation plan reflects what will actually happen in your setting.

Review your church staff structure. If you work with a small staff that relies heavily on volunteers, structure this process to include the key leaders (paid and unpaid) who need to get behind the OTC experience.

Use the same process to adapt the timeline to your setting. Look at the upcoming year to determine when an optimal launch date for your congregation would be. Two logical options would be a September start date (to follow the academic calendar) or a January start date (to follow the calendar year).

Are you ready to move to phase 2?

You'll be ready for phase 2 once you have support from key staff members, the approval from senior leaders to release financial and personnel resources for OTC, and a preliminary implementation plan and timeline that reflect your church's situation. Once these are in hand, you're prepared to move on to phase 2, where you will build a core team of leaders.

PHASE 2 | Build a Leadership Team

CHAPTER

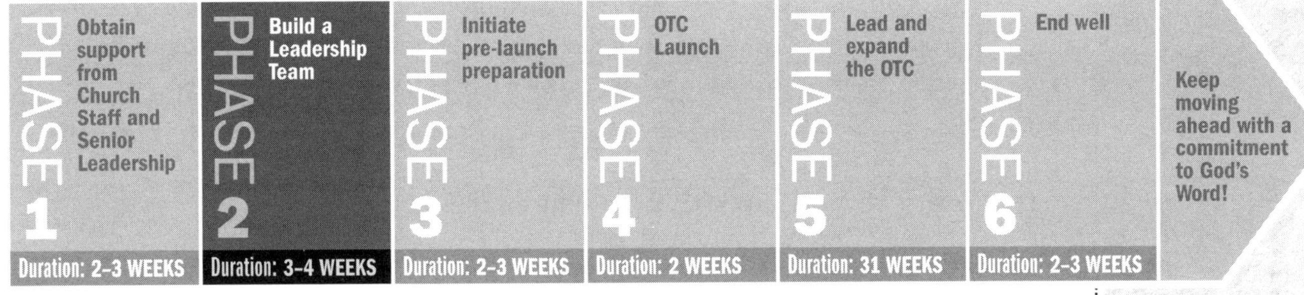

Overview

PURPOSE

The purpose of this phase is to recruit, inspire, and equip the leaders who will launch and maintain a strong Old Testament Challenge experience on all three levels—congregational, small groups, and individual study.

STEPS

In this phase, staff and volunteer leaders are recruited and equipped to lead their unique areas. This includes:

Step 1: Select an Old Testament Challenge core team.
Step 2: Collaborate with the Old Testament Challenge core team to revise and finalize the preliminary implementation plan and timeline.
Step 3: Select and commission an Old Testament Challenge teacher or teaching team.
Step 4: Select and commission volunteers.

IMPORTANCE

Because the Old Testament Challenge is a multilevel, congregation-wide learning experience, effective leadership is essential from beginning to end. For the OTC to have maximum impact, you need a strong team of leaders deeply committed and thoroughly equipped.

CAUTIONS

There are two cautions in this phase. First, all leaders must be committed to full participation in the OTC experience on all three levels—congregational, small group, and individual study. The temptation for some may be to devote themselves to providing leadership for their area alone, to the exclusion of active participation in other areas. To effectively call others to full participation, staff and volunteer leaders must model this commitment themselves.

Second, make every effort to match the right people with the right ministry areas. It is vitally important to match ministry tasks and responsibilities with individuals whose gifts and skills will enable them to do the job well.

Step 1: Select an Old Testament Challenge Core Team

The people who make up your OTC core team must be deeply committed to lead their areas and also fully participate in the OTC experience on all three levels. To help leaders understand the importance of their roles on the OTC core team and to formally secure their commitment, ask them to sign the OTC Leadership Covenant. A copy of the Leadership Covenant is included in the appendix on page 64.

Is it necessary to form a core team?

It is essential! Some programs in a church can just happen spontaneously, but this is not one of them. Because this is a long-term, congregation-wide commitment, a strong core team must be in place from the very beginning. This team is critically important, not only to launch the OTC but also to keep momentum going and to provide direction throughout the experience.

Who should be on the core team?

OTC champion. This person is responsible to lead the core team and consistently uphold the vision and values of the OTC before the congregation. Ideally, the champion should be the primary OTC teacher. The primary teacher will have regular visibility with the congregation, so this is a natural fit. There is a sample ministry position description for the OTC champion in the appendix on page 65.

Congregation point person. This person oversees all aspects of preparing, launching, and maintaining a strong OTC experience at the congregational level. Depending on the size of the church, this could include leading a team of volunteers who take ownership of specific tasks. The congregation point person partners with the OTC champion and others to maximize the OTC learning experience at the congregational level. There is a sample ministry position description for the congregation point person in the appendix on page 66.

Small-group point person. This leader champions the OTC at the small-group level. By recruiting, equipping, and supporting small-group leaders, the point person assures that every person who wants to be in an OTC small group gets connected and has the opportunity to be part of a transforming small-group learning experience. There is a sample ministry position description for the small-group point person in the appendix on page 67.

Programming point person. This person builds a team of volunteers who implement the OTC's unique programming elements. All the programming elements needed to effectively run the OTC—video segments, PowerPoint® presentations, and so on—are included in the four OTC kits. The programming point person shapes these elements to make them fit the unique needs of your church and oversees the technical aspects of implementing them. There is a sample ministry position description for the programming point person in the appendix on page 68.

What is the best way to recruit core team leaders?

Begin with prayer. Ask God to provide strong leaders who will be passionate students of the Old Testament during this whole campaign.

Prepare clear and detailed ministry position descriptions. Use the ministry descriptions mentioned above so those who volunteer for these positions know exactly what commitment they are making.

Have one-on-one meetings with a handful of potential leaders. As you anticipate and pray for the launch of the OTC experience, be mindful of those whose gifts and skills line up with your ministry position descriptions. Set up one-on-one meetings with these individuals and invite them to consider becoming a core team point person.

Recruit throughout the whole church. Make personal contact with those you feel would be effective core team leaders. Meet with them and highlight the life-changing values of the Old Testament Challenge (for the leaders and the church). Keep in mind that even those who do not become part of the core team may be good candidates for other volunteer leadership roles as the OTC experience moves forward.

How do you know when you are ready for step 2?

When your core team members are aware of their responsibilities and committed to the OTC, you are ready to move to the next step.

Step 2: Collaborate with the Old Testament Challenge Core Team to Revise and Finalize the Preliminary Implementation Plan and Timeline

What is the preliminary implementation plan and timeline?

A preliminary implementation plan and timeline is a tool that helps you think through every aspect of launching an effective OTC experience customized for your church. It includes finances, staff and volunteer requirements, target dates for every implementation phase, and more. Although the comprehensive, six-phase implementation plan outlined here will effectively lead you through the process, the OTC champion and core team need to consider carefully how the requirements of each phase will impact the unique circumstances of your staff, volunteers, and congregation. A sample implementation plan and timeline are included in the appendix on page 60.

How often should the core team meet?

Prior to launching the OTC, the core team should meet as often as needed to accomplish all tasks. Once you have a final implementation plan and timeline, then core team point persons begin recruiting volunteers for their areas. Once the OTC is launched, the core team should meet as often as necessary for prayer, ongoing communication, and encouragement.

How do you know when you are ready for step 3?

When your core team has met, agreed on an implementation plan, and set a realistic timeline for your church to walk through the OTC, you are ready to move on to step 3.

Step 3: Select and Commission an Old Testament Challenge Teacher or Teaching Team

Is it better to have one teacher or to use a teaching team?

Both options are fine. In some churches there is just one teaching pastor, so that a team approach is not possible. For churches that have more than one teacher, utilizing a teaching team can be a good option, but one primary teacher for the OTC can also be effective.

Why is it important to commission the OTC leadership team?

The OTC is a powerful experience your church will remember for years to come. Taking time, in a worship service, to commission and pray for your OTC leadership team can be a visible marker that communicates the significance of the event for the whole congregation. During this same service, you may also wish to invite people to sign an OTC covenant, signifying a personal commitment to the Old Testament Challenge. A sample OTC covenant is included in the appendix on page 69.

When is the best time to commission the OTC team?

The best time is during the worship service(s) in which the OTC will be taught in the coming months. This time of commissioning does not need to be long, but it does need to be seen as a significant moment in the life of the church. Simply introducing the team members, announcing their unique area of responsibility in the OTC, and praying for them can be a meaningful experience.

Step 4: Select and Commission Volunteers

How many volunteers are needed?

The number of volunteers needed depends on the size of your church, the number of staff members you can devote to OTC leadership, and the unique needs identified in your implementation plan. It is the responsibility of each core team point person to recruit and lead their volunteer team members throughout the OTC.

You need to form three distinct leadership teams to launch and lead the OTC:

- ***Congregation team.*** Under the leadership of the congregation point person, this team is responsible for promoting, launching, and maintaining momentum at the congregational level.
- ***Small-group team.*** Under the leadership of the small-group point person, this team recruits existing and new small-group leaders, equips them to use the OTC materials, and encourages them throughout the experience. This team is also charged with finding creative ways to inspire and mobilize the maximum number of existing small groups to commit to using the OTC small-group curriculum as well as launching new groups specifically for OTC study.
- ***Programming team.*** Under the leadership of the programming point person, this team has the unique role of being an ongoing resource to the OTC teacher or teaching team. They help implement a variety of creative programming elements and provide all technical support.

What is the best way for core team leaders to recruit leaders for their teams?

See the response to a similar question in step 1 on page 33.

When is the best time to commission the OTC volunteer team?

The best time is during the same worship service in which you plan to pray for your core team. This time of commissioning and prayer can include small-group leaders, the team that will lead the OTC charge in the worship services, your technical team, and anyone else who is committed to help make the OTC a reality for your church.

Are you ready to move to phase 3?

You will be ready to move to the next phase when you have recruited your core team, recruited the other volunteers you will need, established a preliminary implementation plan (including a timeline), and have scheduled and planned a time to commission your OTC leaders. Once these things are done, you are ready to move on to pre-launch preparations.

PHASE 3 | Initiate Pre-Launch Preparation

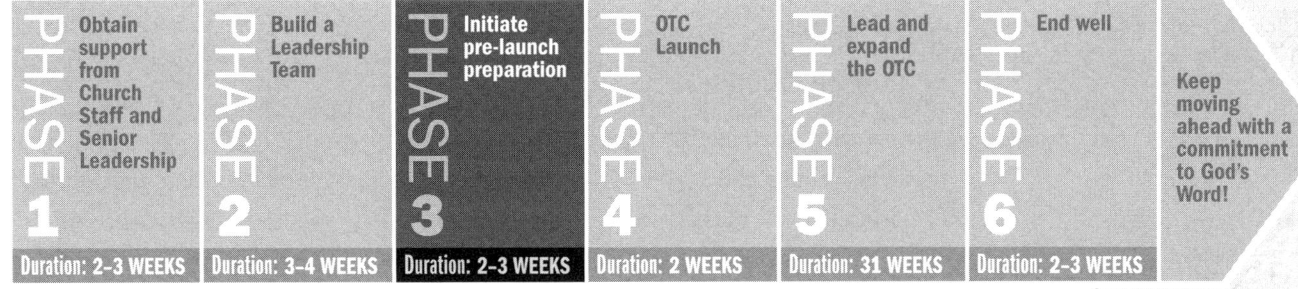

Overview

PURPOSE

The purpose of phase 3 is to do all the necessary preparation work for launching the Old Testament Challenge. This includes casting vision in the congregation, promoting the OTC , and calling the entire congregation to seriously consider the level of commitment they will make to it.

STEPS

The steps you need to take in preparing your congregation to launch the Old Testament Challenge include:

Step 1: Begin pre-launch promotions.
Step 2: Invite the church to take the Old Testament Challenge and secure commitments.
Step 3: Begin pre-launch preparations.

IMPORTANCE

Preparation is essential for the OTC to operate effectively. Because this experience involves commitment on three levels—congregational, small group, and individual—communication and preparation are critical. Also, because this is a thirty-two-week series, launching well sets the tone for the whole experience.

CAUTIONS

Because the Old Testament Challenge is a unique thirty-two-week congregational journey that leads people into three distinct levels of learning, the pre-launch time is very important. Don't rush through this phase. Be sure to do all you can to promote the OTC on all three levels: congregational, small-group, and individual.

Step 1: Begin Pre-launch Promotions

CONGREGATIONAL LEVEL

Your OTC champion is the vital link in communicating with the full congregation. This leader is the primary voice promoting the OTC and sharing the vision for how this journey of learning can impact your whole church. This leader should be given time in your regular worship services to begin communicating about the goals for the OTC. The portion of the OTC that everyone in your congregation will be part of is the congregational level. But this does not mean you don't have to promote this aspect of the OTC. It is still important that there be a sense of anticipation, excitement, and commitment on the part of everyone who attends your church.

Verbal promotions: Have your OTC champion and other members of the OTC leadership team give brief announcements explaining the goals and benefits of taking the Old Testament Challenge. Encourage your full OTC leadership team and all those who will be leading small groups and technical aspects of the OTC experience to begin spreading the word on an interpersonal level. Remember that word-of-mouth promotion is very effective.

Written promotions: Use whatever written communication vehicles your church has in place to promote the OTC. If you have a newsletter, church magazine, or some kind of weekly church update, use these. Also, if you have a church website, get OTC information on it as soon as possible. You might even want to consider sending a personal letter from the OTC champion to everyone who attends your church.

Other creative promotions: Have buttons made for all those who will be leading the OTC that simply say "OTC." Then, wait for people to begin asking what it means. Make OTC posters and tent cards to be set at tables or around the lobby of your church. They can say, "OTC," or "What is the OTC?" or "Coming soon . . . OTC." The key is to create interest and to get people asking questions.

Set up an OTC information center: Establish a place where people can come and get literature or ask questions about the OTC. Plan to keep this information center in a visible place throughout the entire OTC journey. Use good signage and keep it in a place where you get maximum traffic.

Video: At some point in your promotions you might want to use the video segment provided in the OTC resource kit. In this video, John Ortberg casts a vision for the Old Testament Challenge.

Small Groups

Everyone who attends your church will be part of the congregational level of the OTC. The small-group level calls for two specific kinds of promotion.

Promotion among existing small groups: It is important to promote the OTC among existing small groups early in the process. Be sure to get the small-group materials into the hands of group leaders so they can show these to their group members. These group leaders can then help their members see the value of studying the same passages and themes they will be learning about in the church worship services.

Promotion for new groups: Your small-group point person should already be recruiting and preparing leaders for new groups that will focus on the OTC. Be sure to extend verbal and written invitations to all who attend your church. Raise the value of the OTC small-group experience and let everyone know they can be part of a small group. If your church doesn't have a small-group ministry, this could be the perfect opportunity to start one.

Individual

One of the greatest strengths of the Old Testament Challenge is that it provides a way for individuals to dig deeply into God's Word for forty weeks. If people develop a discipline of personal Bible study for this length of time, it could easily become a habit that stays with them for the rest of their lives!

Survey: A Hundred-Question Biblical Literacy Test has been developed for the OTC (provided on the CD-ROM and in the appendix beginning on page 70). While people may be discouraged at their lack of Old Testament knowledge, they're more likely to see their need and be motivated to dig in once the OTC begins. Encourage individuals to take this test on their own to assess their Old Testament knowledge. This same survey can be taken at the end of the OTC to measure growth in biblical literacy.

Level of commitment: The OTC individual reading guide offers two levels of commitment. (1) The first is a high level of challenge that involves six days of reading and reflection each week. This option leads participants through a process of reading the entire Old Testament in forty weeks. (2) The second option provides a reading guide for three days a week and covers many major texts and themes in the Old Testament, but it does not encompass the entire Old Testament. Make copies of the reading guide available at your OTC information booth. Be sure to let people know that there are two options for the individual reading element of the OTC.

Bookmark: Create a bookmark for participants. Both Willow Creek and Corinth Reformed Church created an OTC bookmark as a small promotional tool to encourage personal study. Willow's bookmark had the reading schedule on it. Corinth's had the books of the Old Testament in order and also included a few themes to look for in the Old Testament (as suggested in the first OTC message).

Step 2: Invite the Church to Take the Old Testament Challenge and Secure Commitments

After a period of focused promotion, it is time to ask people what level of commitment they want to make to the OTC. This needs to be done during a worship service. This will do two things: It will make a clear statement that this is a congregation-wide event and that everyone is invited, and it will allow everyone to respond and turn in a commitment card.

OTC commitment card: The OTC commitment card (see page 69 in the appendix) will provide space for people to respond on all three levels. These cards should be distributed to everyone as they enter. During the service, have everyone fill in the card and indicate if they will:

- commit to attend church regularly for the coming thirty-two weeks and prayerfully listen and learn from the messages.
- commit to become part of an OTC small group.
- commit to participate in the OTC individual reading plan.

Once the cards are filled in, ask that these be placed in the offering plates or passed to where ushers will pick them up.

Begin an OTC database: All of the commitment cards need to be entered into your church computer database. This list will be helpful as you determine how many small groups you need to start. It will help you plan to order sufficient small-group studies and individual reading guides. It will also be helpful if you want to send out an occasional postcard encouraging those who are taking the OTC to stay the course and hang in there to the end of the race!

Communication with those not present: Because commitment to the OTC is so important, your team might want to communicate with all those who are not in attendance (or who don't fill in an OTC commitment card) and let them know that they are invited to be part of the OTC as well. You could send a letter sharing the vision and including the commitment card and then provide a place where they can turn in this card at the OTC information center (or provide registration on your website). You could also make an announcement the following week, for those who missed that week, that you did this as a congregation. Mailing this card to all those not present is also valuable because people in your church who are at home recovering from a surgery or are shut-ins can accept the challenge as well. Also, those who may have drifted away from regular attendance might feel a prompting from the Holy Spirit and consider reconnecting in the life of the church during the OTC.

Step 3: Begin Pre-Launch Preparations

When you have effectively promoted the OTC and secured commitments from the full congregation, you are ready to begin the next step of practical preparations to launch the OTC . Here are some key preparations that need to be made:

Begin forming small groups: Give your OTC small-group point person the list of all who want to be part of new OTC small groups and begin work on forming groups so that everyone will be included.

Order OTC materials: Both the small-group study guide and the individual reading guide can be purchased through your local Christian bookstore. Materials can also be purchased directly from Zondervan or the Willow Creek Association:

Zondervan ChurchSource
(800) 727-3480 / www.ZondervanChurchSource.com

Willow Creek Direct
(800) 570-9812 / www.willowcreek.com

Call your chosen supplier in advance to determine how much lead time you need to order materials and receive them on time. Be sure they are in the hands of your church members and leaders before you launch the OTC.

Payment for OTC materials: You need to determine the best way to handle the cost of OTC materials. Here are some options:

- Pay for all resources out of an OTC church budget. Your church can decide to incur all costs of supplying small-group guides and individual reading guides for those who take the OTC and mark a commitment card indicating a desire to be in a small group or to do the individual reading. Depending on the size of your church, this could be a substantial financial commitment. If you choose this option, you need to have a team at your OTC information center distributing all resources prior to launch.
- Share the cost with participants. After ordering sufficient resources, invite people to pick up their resources at the OTC information center and to pay for them then. If you choose this option, you need to provide a team to handle distribution and financial logistics. It is preferable for people to incur the cost themselves. This helps them to take the challenges more seriously when they have invested their money as well as their time.
- Create your own option. The key is to make sure all materials are ordered, distributed, and paid for before the official OTC launch.

Are you ready to move to phase 4?

When you have effectively promoted the Old Testament Challenge through your whole congregation, invited everyone to participate, secured commitments, and made pre-launch preparations, you are ready to move to phase 4 and launch the OTC.

CHAPTER 7

PHASE 4 | Old Testament Challenge Launch

PHASE 2 — Build a Leadership Team — Duration: 3–4 WEEKS

PHASE 3 — Initiate pre-launch preparation — Duration: 2–3 WEEKS

PHASE 4 — OTC Launch — Duration: 2 WEEKS

PHASE 5 — Lead and expand the OTC — Duration: 31 WEEKS

PHASE 6 — End well — Duration: 2–3 WEEKS

Keep moving ahead with a commitment to God's Word!

Overview

PURPOSE

The purpose of phase 4 is to launch all three levels of the OTC (congregation, small groups, and individual study) with excitement and momentum.

STEPS

The steps in launching the Old Testament Challenge are:

Step 1: Plan ahead to make the first week run smoothly.
Step 2: Begin the Old Testament Challenge individual reading program.
Step 3: Begin teaching the Old Testament Challenge to the congregation in the weekly services.
Step 4: Begin studying the Old Testament Challenge in small groups.

IMPORTANCE

Starting well is critical for any event in the church. But starting a thirty-two-week process of studying through the Old Testament as a congregation, small groups, and individuals must be done well. This first week sets the tone for the entire Old Testament Challenge, and starting well will help you launch with excitement and energy.

CAUTION

The launch of the OTC is not a single launch of one rocket booster; it is a multiple booster launch. You start the congregational study, the OTC small groups, and the individual reading all the same week. The primary caution at this point is to make sure all materials are in hand, all congregational commitments are made, and everything launches simultaneously.

Step 1: Plan Ahead to Make the First Week Run Smoothly

There are a number of important tasks for the week leading up to the OTC launch. Gather your core team and be sure everyone is tracking together. Here are some areas to focus during the final preparation week:

Pray: Gather various groups to pray for God's blessing on the OTC experience. You may want to have prayer time with the OTC core team, your church board, your staff, and the entire congregation the week prior to the launch. Stress the great potential for changed lives through in-depth study of God's Word. Pray for a powerful movement of God in preparation for the OTC launch.

Promote: Continue to promote the whole experience, with emphasis on the individual reading program. Let those who have not yet committed to the OTC know that it is not too late. Have additional commitment cards available at the OTC information center. Provide a basket or box where people can turn in their cards. Be sure someone checks the basket or box regularly and notifies the OTC small-group point person if there are additional people who want to be in a group.

Meet: Be sure you meet as an OTC core team the week before the launch and review the timetable. The key is to make sure everyone is ready for the launch and that all the details are covered.

Step 2: Begin the Old Testament Challenge Individual Reading Program

At this point, many in your congregation will have made a commitment to do one of the two reading programs for the OTC. Here are some details to keep in mind as you move them into their individual OTC reading guides:

- The first week of reading should be completed by the time people come to hear the first OTC message. This means you need to distribute the individual reading guides at least a full week in advance of this date. Be sure everyone has their reading guide and knows that it is ideal to start reading one full week prior to the first OTC message.

- New people will be coming to your church through the whole OTC process, and many will want to jump in right where you are. Be sure to have additional copies of the reading guide available at the OTC information center.
- During the first OTC service, the OTC champion should give a word of encouragement to those who have started their reading.

Step 3: Begin Teaching Old Testament Challenge to the Congregation in the Weekly Services

The OTC champion should be ready to teach and lead the first OTC service. Here are some important reminders:

- It is vital that the programming point person be aware of any special needs, such as use of video, props, and stage set-up. This person can work with all the technical elements of the service so that the OTC champion can focus on teaching.
- The first message sets the tone for the remainder of the OTC experience. The OTC champion needs to be prepared and prayerful. This could be one of the most important messages he or she will bring over the next thirty-two weeks!

Step 4: Begin Studying the Old Testament Challenge in Small Groups

The small-group element comes as the third rocket booster to hit in the OTC launch. First, people begin their individual reading. Next, the congregational study is introduced. Third, in the week following the first OTC message, small groups begin to meet. Here are some thoughts on the launch of small groups:

- Each small-group leader needs to decide when to distribute the study guides—either at the first OTC group meeting or in advance so members can have time to look over the first session. This should be decided by the OTC small-group point person and the small-group leaders.
- OTC small groups are designed to key off of weekly messages, so groups need to meet every week in which there is an OTC message. Groups using the OTC curriculum need to meet on a schedule that follows the OTC teaching schedule.
- There are some weeks in which an OTC message won't be taught. For example, your church may break from the Old Testament Challenge during the Christmas or Easter seasons or

for other special services. When this happens, it is important to schedule those weeks off from small-group study. Groups can still meet, of course, but they will not want to press on with the next week of study since it is designed to parallel the message in the worship service. The OTC champion and the OTC small-group point person will need to communicate well in advance which weeks will be "break weeks" from the OTC teaching and small-group studies.

Once you are past the first week of the OTC and the congregational, small-group, and individual levels of the program are launched, you are ready to move to phase 5.

PHASE 5 | Lead and Expand the Old Testament Challenge

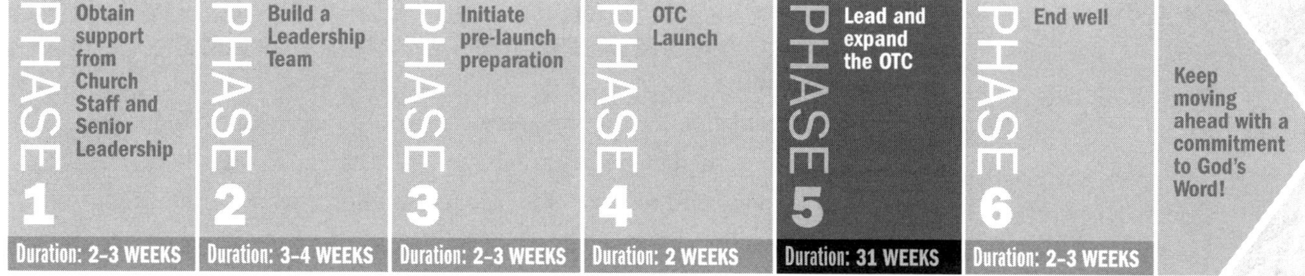

Overview

PURPOSE

The purpose of phase 5 is to keep the momentum of the Old Testament Challenge going strong through solid leadership, which will expand the impact of each resource on the church.

STEPS

The steps involved with leading and expanding the Old Testament Challenge are:

Step 1: Keep leaders on track.
Step 2: Plan for smooth transitions from kit to kit.
Step 3: Maintain momentum and excitement.

IMPORTANCE

Although the OTC teaching is fresh and offers new themes and ideas each week, the OTC run is long! Strong enthusiasm in the beginning stages needs to be reinforced throughout the entire experience to help leaders and participants maintain momentum and commitment.

CAUTIONS

The "living out" of the OTC is highly individual for each church. Therefore, the most important thing you can do at this stage is to ask and answer some assessment questions that spur your thinking on ways to build and maintain momentum for your people. Several creative ideas are also offered here, but keep in mind that the ongoing input and discernment of your core team is essential during this phase.

Step 1: Keep Leaders on Track

Core team: The core team established during phase 2 should continue to meet as frequently as needed to assure clear communication about what's coming in future weeks and how it impacts each area: congregational, small groups, individuals, communications staff, support staff, and so on. Initially, for example, weekly meetings are probably required until a clear rhythm of planning for future services and transitions has been established. After that, a monthly meeting of the core team may suffice.

Congregational: Those who plan services should meet weekly. Their goal in this phase is to help the congregation remain motivated and clear about the "why" of what they're doing and to make sure services reinforce what people are experiencing in both small groups and individual reading.

Small groups: Small-group leaders can be kept on track in various ways. If you have e-mail access to your leaders, send periodic e-mails to encourage them and remind them of the great value of what they are doing. Use the main service as an opportunity to encourage and support those who lead small groups. Be sure to highlight their role and the important part they play in helping the church integrate the truths taught in the main services.

Individuals: If your church asked people to sign a formal commitment to read through the Old Testament, then it is appropriate and beneficial to contact these people during the year to encourage them in their reading and personal study. You can do this by e-mail, by a postcard, or by phone contact.

Step 2: Plan for Smooth Transitions from Kit to Kit

There are four OTC kits, and the transition point from one kit to the next is significant at all three levels.

Congregational: Each transition point marks progress and should be noted and celebrated during the main services. Additionally, those who plan these services will need the next kit in advance so they can plan their future work accordingly.

Small groups: With each transition to a new teaching kit, there is a corresponding transition for small groups to the next curriculum. Thus, there needs to be a clear plan to secure and distribute the next curriculum in advance so the transition to new material is smooth and seamless. Be sure to always have additional small-group study guides available at your OTC information center.

Individuals: The introduction of a new kit and corresponding small-group curriculum do not require anything new of those who are already keeping up with the reading plan. However, the transition does provide a natural opportunity to recruit newcomers to the reading plan. Invite them to pick up right where you are in the OTC. Be sure to always have additional individual reading guides available at your OTC information center.

Who needs what, and when do they need it?

Congregational: Those who plan the main services need the new kit at least three weeks in advance of the first message in that kit. For example, if you are in kit 1, you should have kit 2 in hand by the time you reach session 7 (of the nine sessions in kit 1).

Small groups: Small groups need to have their new curriculum the week before the new kit starts. To transition to kit 2, small-group members need their curriculum by session 9 of kit 1. Plan ahead so you know how many copies of the curriculum you need to have ready by session 9. Have someone order the correct number of copies and make sure there is a system in place to distribute these materials and also to collect payment if needed. Be sure to take advantage of the fact that each transition to a new kit provides small groups with a natural opportunity to invite new people into existing small groups or to launch new groups.

Individuals: Make sure you have sufficient copies of the reading guides on hand for people to begin their reading plan midway through the year. The transition to a new kit provides an ideal opportunity to invite people to join in the challenge.

How will people get what they need?

Don't be caught off guard by the completion of a kit! Determine your strategy for securing the necessary OTC resources well in advance so everyone who is impacted by the introduction of a new kit—especially those who lead the main services and those who lead small groups—will get exactly what they need when they need it. These questions can help you develop your strategy for a successful transition:

- Who is responsible for tallying how many copies of the curriculum are needed?
- Who is responsible for ordering the next kit?
- How far in advance do resources need to be ordered to arrive on time?
- How will curriculum copies be distributed to small-group leaders?

Be bluntly clear and straightforward in telling people exactly what is involved in getting what they need on time. Be ruthlessly proactive in communicating the dates and processes for securing all resources.

Step 3: Maintain Momentum and Excitement

CONGREGATIONAL

Ask your core team to consider these questions:

- What will motivate your congregation to keep going?
- What will bring a sense of momentum to their efforts?
- What will challenge them to live out the things they are learning?

Here are three ideas to motivate and challenge your church:

Scripture service: Devote a portion of the main service to allowing individuals to share Scriptures that have been significant to them during the OTC up to this point. Set up one or more open microphones in the congregation and invite people to share a verse or short passage of Scripture that has impacted them deeply. Ask participants to share only the verse or passage. No comments are necessary in order for this to be a deeply moving experience for the community.

Learn from the prophets: During the final message series the congregation is challenged to develop a heart of compassion for the marginalized and underprivileged in society, just as the Minor Prophets challenged Israel to share God's heart and desire to care for widows and orphans. Allow your congregation to wrestle with what it would mean to live out the "plumb line" introduced by Amos or to "desire mercy and not sacrifice" as commanded by Micah. Consider launching a church-wide effort to extend practical care to the underprivileged in your community, taking up the challenge not only to learn from the prophets but also to live out the values they taught.

Use miniseries breaks to mark progress: Throughout the Old Testament Challenge, the messages are grouped into several miniseries. Use the transition points between miniseries to mark significant learning from the series just completed and to cast vision for what will be introduced in the series to come. Include not only the biblical truths covered but also the connections these truths have to our lives as Christ-followers today. Remember, the OTC is broken into four sections, based on the four kits. The basic breakdown is:

- Kit 1: The Pentateuch
- Kit 2: The History of Israel
- Kit 3: The Wisdom Literature
- Kit 4: The Prophets

These divisions form natural times to celebrate, look back, and anticipate what lies ahead.

Visual markers: Create a visual representation to mark your progress through the Old Testament. As you complete each major section of Scripture, choose a symbol to represent that portion and place it on a visual timeline that will expand as the OTC unfolds. It can be shown in a variety of ways, whether on slides or actually on display somewhere in the church. Examples of symbols would be tablets signifying the introduction of the Ten Commandments or a pillar of fire for Israel's time in the wilderness. A scale could represent the period of the judges, while a crown the time of the kings. These visual reminders celebrate the passing of significant milestones and help people see and appreciate the progress they've made as the OTC continues.

Small Groups

Small groups can build a sense of momentum in a variety of ways. Some ideas include:

Small-group leader retreat: Plan a retreat for small-group leaders. Your primary goal in the retreat is to encourage and develop leadership skills. This would be a great time to survey leaders to learn what benefits their groups have derived from studying the Old Testament together, as well as the value of the integrated approach in the OTC. Questions could include:

- What has been the greatest benefit of the OTC to your small group?
- What has been the greatest benefit to you personally?
- What has been the greatest challenge during the OTC for your group?

Sharing: Share what you learn about what's happening in small groups with the whole church, either through the main service or through another communication channel. This will allow those who are involved in small groups to see the progress being made in other small groups and thus be motivated to continue and keep pursuing their own spiritual growth with great intensity.

The power of one person sharing his or her story can provide a momentum-building experience for anyone in a small group. As you learn of those whose lives have been deeply touched by their OTC small-group experience, it can motivate others in small groups to hear these stories. This could happen through a main service or at a gathering of those in small groups created especially to celebrate progress made thus far and to cast vision for the rest of the series.

Favorite verse in each book: As the group moves through each book of the Old Testament, have group members identify their favorite verse from each book and write it on an index card to give to the group leader. The leader can create a book, like a photo album, that keeps all of these verses throughout the year. At the end of the year, the group decides whether to keep the book as it is or to give back to each individual his or her cards with favorite verses. Groups who do this find that the book becomes a periodic reminder of key truths they have been touched by, and it encourages them to continue on.

Individuals

Keeping the vision strong for individuals is so important! Maintain momentum by acknowledging the reading plan(s) during services throughout the year. The teacher(s) at these services can ask questions such as these:

- How are you doing with the reading?
- How's everyone liking Leviticus?
- Who was surprised by the Song of Solomon this week?

It becomes a subtheme throughout the year since it is assumed that the majority of people are reading along in the Old Testament.

Amnesty service: To keep expectations realistic and help motivate people to keep reading, introduce an amnesty service in which people who have fallen behind in the reading receive amnesty and feel free to join the reading plan as scheduled, regardless of how far behind they have fallen. Even if they stopped reading somewhere in Exodus, encourage people to stay current with the reading for this week's service and to join in the challenge from this point forward.

Some new people may have joined your congregation since the OTC was launched, and this is an opportunity to invite them to join in the challenge. When you do this, be sure to direct them to the OTC information center so they can fill in a commitment card and pick up the resources they need.

PHASE 6 | End Well

CHAPTER

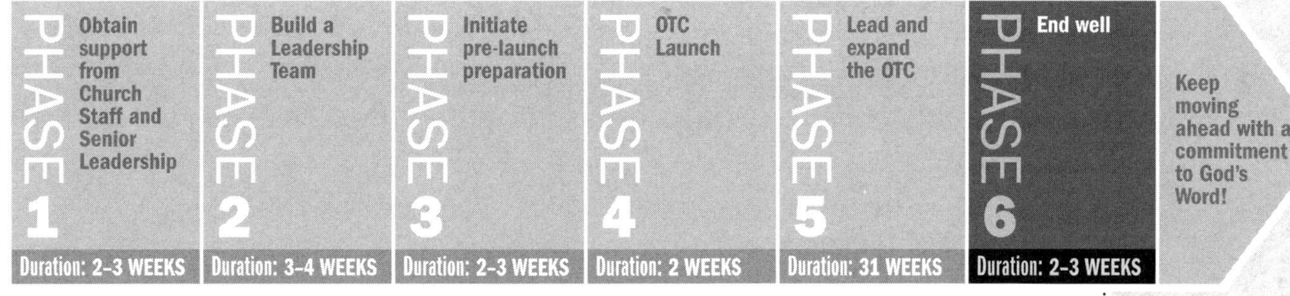

Overview

PURPOSE

The purpose of phase 6 is to provide a strong sense of closure and accomplishment by celebrating all that God has done and by evaluating the effectiveness of the OTC experience at every level.

STEPS

Steps involved in ending well are:

Step 1: Celebrate the experience.
Step 2: Evaluate.
Step 3: Move ahead with a commitment to God's Word.

IMPORTANCE

You and your church have learned so much, have worked so hard, and have grown in community and in your relationship with God. Now it's time to *celebrate!* Marking this achievement allows you to recognize all that has happened and the many benefits that all this work has brought to you. It is also a crucial time to ask for honest evaluation from everyone involved so you can both celebrate well and better meet spiritual growth needs in the future.

CAUTIONS

Some individuals may still be reading when the thirty-two weeks of teaching conclude. Be sure to acknowledge and validate the heroic reading efforts that have been made thus far. You may want to choose an additional celebration time when individuals following the forty-week plan finally finish the entire Old Testament, though because of holiday breaks and other special services, the forty-week readers may be completing their reading assignments at the same time the whole church OTC teaching ends.

While affirming the sense of accomplishment that many may feel, continue to emphasize the primary value that people are actually growing in their relationship with God. What God is most interested in is not what we've accomplished but rather who we've become. We learn and study so we can become more loving—more like Christ. Keep this vision at the forefront—that we have learned these things in order to know our God, then serve more willingly, love more freely, and give more generously. We are being shaped and formed by the Scriptures that shaped and formed Jesus.

Step 1: Celebrate the Experience

Why celebrate?

Too often it is our habit to move on quickly in life—we're always in a hurry. This is not the case with God, and it's not healthy for the development of the human soul. In fact, a big theme in the early part of the OTC is the celebrating heart of our great God—entire chapters of the Pentateuch are devoted to teaching the nation of Israel to celebrate. Apply what you've learned by creating ways for your church to finish well with an emphasis on joy and celebration.

What are some ways to celebrate?

Congregational: Devote a final service to celebrating the Old Testament Challenge. Creatively recap central themes, share personal stories, and acknowledge those who finished the reading guide. One way to acknowledge those who have done the reading is to have everyone stand who read along in the Old Testament with the reading guide and cheer for them! You can also ask, "And how many of you have read more of the Old Testament than ever before in your life?" Almost everyone will stand here, and the applause should be thunderous!

Small groups: Plan an OTC party to gather those who built community through small groups during the OTC. They could have a time of prayer in groups and sharing about what was most meaningful to them during their study. You might want to recap some of the lessons from session 9 in kit 1. This is the session where you studied God's desire for his children to celebrate with feasts and festivals. Be sure to have good food and a time of feasting and celebration!

Individuals: Encourage individuals who completed the OTC reading to mark their accomplishment in some formal way. Have them mark the actual completion date in the last page of the Old Testament in their Bible, noting perhaps the first time they read through the Old Testament. Urge them to pray a prayer of worship and thanksgiving to God. Individuals can also retake the "Hundred-Question Biblical Literacy Test." By taking the test a second time, they can test their new knowledge!

Leadership team: Throw a party for the staff and volunteers who worked so hard to lead and facilitate the Old Testament Challenge. All those meetings, all those prayers, all those decisions, all those last-minute emergencies—in the end, they were all a team effort to help the church grow spiritually. This is worth both acknowledging and celebrating! And the joy of doing great work together should not be taken for granted.

Let the people you serve alongside know you care about them and value them and are grateful to God for their contribution to the kingdom. Your thoughts toward them could be communicated through handwritten notes, through words of praise and thanks during the party, or simply in conversation. Be sure to thank everyone who served, and help them to see how God has worked powerfully through their efforts.

Step 2: Evaluate the OTC Experience

We often make assumptions about what people think or how they feel about their experiences. We project our own ideas, make inferences, or take one or two informal conversations to be reflective of the whole. The best way to get to truth is to ask for it. In an effort to end well, give your congregation the opportunity to voice their perspectives on the overall experience.

Paper or web surveys are usually the best way to get answers to these questions, and, when asked in the right way, surveys can provide very valuable information.

Congregation: On a survey like this, the ideal questions are yes/no or multiple choice, so the results can be quickly tallied and reported.

Sample survey:

For each question, circle the number or word that best describes your response.

- How much did you grow in your understanding of what the Old Testament teaches?

  1 **2** **3** **4** **5**

  Not at all ... Very much

- How much did you grow in your relationship with God through the OTC?

  1 **2** **3** **4** **5**

  Not at all ... Very much

- Were you involved in a small group that studied the OTC?

  Yes **No**

- Did you participate in the reading for the OTC?

  Yes **No**

- How much of the individual reading plan did you complete for the OTC?

  1 **2** **3** **4** **5**

  None All

- Which statement best describes the greatest benefit to you from the OTC (choose one):

  ☐ I have a better understanding of and appreciation for the Old Testament.

  ☐ My small group experience deepened my understanding and helped me to apply Old Testament teachings in my daily life.

  ☐ I gained a greater sense of community because we learned together as a church.

  ☐ Other: ______________________________

Small groups: As a subgroup of the entire congregation, small groups can help you learn much about the effectiveness of the OTC experience. They can tell you important things about what actually happened in those groups and what they'd like to see in the future. So invite their input.

Sample survey:

For each statement, circle the number that best describes your response.

- Learning the same thing in church and my small group enhanced the spiritual growth of those in the group.

  1 **2** **3** **4** **5**

  Strongly disagree Strongly agree

- My faith and personal life have been shaped by the truths I've learned through the Old Testament Challenge.

  1 **2** **3** **4** **5**

  Strongly disagree Strongly agree

- I would like to continue learning by integrating congregational teaching with the small-group experience in the future.

  1 **2** **3** **4** **5**

  Strongly disagree Strongly agree

Leadership: It is vital to get feedback from key staff members and volunteers. Use open-ended questions that lend themselves to discussion. Have people answer questions on their own before coming to a meeting where these questions can be discussed and the team can hear from one another.

Consider asking questions like these:

- What was the greatest benefit of the OTC?
- Where did we see the greatest impact or life change? Why?
- What was the greatest barrier we encountered while implementing the OTC?
- What did we learn about ourselves?
- What did we learn about God's involvement at our church?
- What did we learn that should influence the way we operate in the future?

Surveys are only effective and useful when those in leadership make a commitment to allow the results to inform their future direction. If formal evaluation and review is a new thing for your church, take advantage of the OTC evaluation process to begin a regular practice of asking your people for information you'd like to know moving forward. This discipline will be helpful to you in a variety of ways in the future, and your congregation will be glad to contribute as they share their insights and experiences.

Step 3: Move Ahead with a Commitment to God's Word

The end of the Old Testament Challenge marks the end of what will be a significant chapter in your church's history. Lives have been changed through the focus provided in the integrated approach to learning and through where you have combined the powerful proclamation of truth in main services, the application in personal lives offered in small groups, and the intensity of personal study. But more than anything else, the church has been immersed in Scripture.

Passages that at one time may have been confusing or unclear have now become life-changing truths that are deeply embedded in our lives. That kind of real-life, intense learning—of deep devotion to and immersion in God's Word—should remain a top priority for your church if you want to continue on the path of spiritual formation towards Christlikeness. Let it be clear from main services and in small groups that the resolve to seek God in his Word will remain solidly in place. As one final challenge, ask the congregation to memorize one verse together that will reflect this commitment to God and to his Word. A few examples of verses you might choose include: Joshua 1:8; Psalm 119:32; Psalm 119:45; Psalm 119:52; Hebrews 4:12. This community-wide experience will foster the sense of ongoing commitment that you share.

This is the perfect time to challenge your congregation to continue with personal disciplines of Bible study on a daily basis and to commit to community in the context of a small group. God has begun a great work in many lives; be proactive in charting a strategy to continue in your devotion to God and commitment to his Word.

APPENDIXES

The appendix contains the following forms and documents to assist you in launching and leading your OTC experience. These documents may be photocopied.

Timeline and Preliminary Implementation Plan

PHASE 1	PHASE 2	PHASE 3	PHASE 4	PHASE 5	PHASE 6	
Obtain support from Church Staff and Senior Leadership	Build a Leadership Team	Initiate pre-launch preparation	OTC Launch	Lead and expand the OTC	End well	Keep moving ahead with a commitment to God's Word!
Duration: 2-3 WEEKS	Duration: 3-4 WEEKS	Duration: 2-3 WEEKS	Duration: 2 WEEKS	Duration: 31 WEEKS	Duration: 2-3 WEEKS	

OTC Checklist

Step	Responsibility of	Target Date	Actual Date	Completion
Phase 1: Obtain Support from Church Staff and Senior Church Leaders				
1 Present OTC vision to church staff and secure support				
2 Present OTC vision to senior church leaders and secure support				
3 Create preliminary implementation plan and timeline				
Phase 2: Build a Leadership Team				
1 Select an OTC core team				
2 Collaborate with OTC core team to revise and finalize the preliminary implementation plan and timeline				
3 Select and commission OTC teacher(s)				
4 Select and commission volunteers				
Phase 3: Initiate Pre-Launch Preparation				
1 Begin pre-launch promotions				
2 Invite the church to take the OTC and secure commitments				
3 Begin pre-launch preparations				
Phase 4: OTC Launch				
1 Plan ahead to make the first week run smoothly				
2 Begin OTC individual study program				
3 Begin teaching the OTC to the congregation in the weekly services				
4 Begin studying the OTC in small groups				
Phase 5: Lead and Expand the OTC				
1 Keep leaders on track				
2 Plan for smooth transitions from kit to kit				
3 Maintain momentum and excitement				
Phase 6: End Well				
1 Celebrate the experience				
2 Evaluate				
3 Move ahead with commitment to God's word				

Financial Worksheets

Use the charts and formulas below to help develop a preliminary budget for OTC expenses.

OTC Kits

In the chart on the right, insert the estimated purchase price (including shipping costs) for each OTC kit:

ITEM	ESTIMATED COST
Kit 1: The Pentateuch (Sessions 1-9)	$
Kit 2: The History of Israel (Sessions 10-16)	$
Kit 3: The Wisdom Literature (Sessions 17-24)	$
Kit 4: The Prophets (Sessions 25-32)	$
KIT COST SUBTOTAL	$

OTC Small Group Study Books

There is one small-group study book corresponding to each of the four OTC kits (listed above). Every person participating in an OTC small group needs to have one small-group study book for each kit (a total of four study books per person over the entire OTC experience). It is recommended that the costs for small group study books be passed along to small-group participants. If you do pass costs along to participants, list the cost in any budget summary you present, but be sure to note that the bottom line impact is "0."

Use the three formulas on the right to estimate the total number of small-group study books needed for existing and new small group participants.

Number of Existing Small Groups	X	Average Number of People in Each Small Group	=	Total Number of Existing Small Group Participants	X .751[1] =	Estimated Small Group Study Books Needed for Existing Small Group Participants
______	X	______	=	______	X .751 =	______

[1]This multiplier signifies a 75 percent participation rate of existing small group members. You may wish to adjust this percentage up or down depending on your expectations.

Estimated Number of New OTC Small Groups	X	Estimated Number of People in Each New Small Group	=	Estimated Small Group Study Books Needed for New Small Group Participants
______	X	______	=	______

Estimated Small Group Study Books Needed for Existing Small Group Participants	+	Estimated Small Group Study Books Needed for New Small Group Participants	=	Small Group Books Needed Per OTC Kit	X 4 OTC Kits	=	Total Quantity of Small Group Study Books Needed for the Entire OTC Experience
______	+	______	=	______	X 4	=	______

Using the total quantity from the formula above as the first number in the formula below, estimate the total cost of small-group study books needed for the entire OTC experience.

Total Small Group Books Needed for the Entire OTC Experience	X	Unit Cost for 1 Book	=	Total Cost of Small Group Study Books for the Entire OTC Experience
______	X	______	=	$ ______

Financial Worksheets

OTC Individual Reading Guides

There is one individual reading guide for the entire OTC experience. It is recommended that the cost for the reading guides be passed along to participants. If you do pass costs along to participants, list the cost in any budget summary you present, but be sure to note that the bottom line impact is "0."

Use the two formulas below to estimate the total number of individual reading guides needed for the entire OTC experience.

Total Number of Students and Adults in the Church	X	.60[2]	=	Total Quantity of Individual Reading Guides Needed for the Entire OTC Experience
______	X	.60	=	$ ______

[2]This multiplier signifies a 60 percent participation rate. You may wish to adjust this percentage up or down depending on your expectations.

Using the total quantity from the formula above as the first number in the formula below, estimate the total cost of individual reading guides needed for the entire OTC experience.

Total Individual Reading Guides Needed for the Entire OTC Experience	X	Unit Cost for 1 Guide	=	Total Cost of Individual Reading Guides for the Entire OTC Experience
______	X	______	=	$ ______

Miscellaneous Costs

In addition to costs for OTC components, it is wise to consider other expenses related to creating an effective OTC experience. These could include things like publicity (printing brochures, tent cards, etc.), programming resources (props or platform artwork), and celebrations (food and decorations). Estimate any miscellaneous expenses below.

ITEM	ESTIMATED COST
	$
	$
	$
	$
	$
	$
	$
	$
	$
	$
MISCELLANEOUS COSTS SUBTOTAL	$

Tally Total Expenses

Using total costs from the charts above, tally total expenses for the OTC experience. Be sure to note any expenses that will be effectively reimbursed when participants purchase their resources.

ITEM	INITIAL COST	FINAL COST
OTC Kit(s)	$	$
Small Group Study Books	$	$
Individual Reading Guides	$	$
Miscellaneous Expenses	$	$
OTC TOTAL COSTS		$

OTC Vision Overview

What is the Old Testament Challenge?

The Old Testament Challenge has been created to help local churches and followers of Christ *discover the life-changing relevance of God's Word.* Particularly, it is designed to move an entire congregation deeply into the two-thirds of the Bible that are often overlooked, the Old Testament.

What is the goal of the OTC?

The Old Testament Challenge will increase biblical literacy and promote spiritual formation by providing church-wide immersion in the Old Testament. This is accomplished through an integrated experience combining congregational teaching, small-group discussion, and individual study so participants experience authentic spiritual growth and churches experience a deeper sense of community. Here is an overview of the three levels of the integrated experience:

Congregation: thirty-two-week message series of relevant teaching through the Old Testament

Small groups: thirty-two-week curriculum based on themes introduced in weekly services

Individuals: individuals reading through the Old Testament Scriptures and interacting with the text in one of two ways:

- thirty-two-week reading guide based on themes introduced in the weekly service
- forty-week reading guide for the entire Old Testament

What is involved in implementing the Old Testament Challenge?

The OTC involves the contribution of several key staff and volunteers, including those who plan and execute congregational services, those who lead and influence small groups and adult learning, those who coordinate church communications, and many others.

What are the benefits of participating in the OTC?

- increased biblical literacy
- increased spiritual growth
- increased sense of community as the entire church studies and grows together
- increased retention of knowledge as weekly church teaching is reinforced in small groups and individual reading

What resources are needed to implement the OTC?

Personnel: dedicated efforts from staff and volunteers in diverse ministry areas such as those who lead the main services and those who influence small groups

Financial: you will incur costs for one or more of the following:

- OTC Kits 1–4
- Small-Group Study Books[3]
- Individual Reading Guides
- Miscellaneous expenses for things such as publicity (brochures or other printed matter), celebrations (refreshments and decorations), and so on

How much time is needed to launch and implement the OTC?

Approximately eleven months: seven to ten weeks to launch, thirty-one weeks to complete, and two to three weeks to conclude well.

[3]One small-group study book and one individual reading guide is included in each kit. Additional copies are purchased separately. It is recommended that costs for the small group study books and individual reading guides be passed along to participants.

LEADERSHIP COVENANT

AS A MEMBER OF THE OTC

LEADERSHIP TEAM I COMMIT TO:

- Pray faithfully for our OTC teacher(s).
- Attend the leadership meetings and contribute with the gifts God has given me.
- Lead my area of the OTC with joy and diligence.
- Attend the weekly OTC services with an open heart to learn.
- Participate in an OTC small group.
- Do my best to finish either the forty-week "full-version" reading guide or the thirty-two-week "fast-track" reading guide.

SIGNED: ______________________________ DATE: __________

Ministry Position Description for OTC Champion

The OTC champion is responsible for leading the OTC core team and consistently upholding the vision and values of the OTC before the congregation. Ideally, the champion is the primary OTC teacher.

Responsibilities

- Schedule and lead all OTC core team meetings as needed (throughout each phase of the OTC experience). This includes going through the *Implementation Guide* as a core team and deciding which areas of responsibility each person will lead.
- Work with the OTC core team to lay out an implementation plan and timeline.
- Keep lines of communication open with the OTC programming point person to assure that all OTC messages and congregational gatherings have what they need to run smoothly.
- Give consistent encouragement to all OTC participants during worship services throughout the OTC.
- Prepare and present the weekly OTC messages. This can be done by one person or by a teaching team.

Ministry Position Description for Congregational Point Person

The congregational point person oversees all aspects of preparing, launching, and maintaining a strong OTC experience at the congregational level. This includes a range of tasks, such as leading teams of volunteers and partnering with the OTC champion and others to maximize the OTC learning experience at the congregational level. Note that the point person is responsible for making sure these tasks are accomplished, though specific responsibilities for various tasks may be delegated to others.

Responsibilities

- Recruit a team (or multiple teams) of volunteers to implement the OTC experience. The team should be customized to your church size and worship service needs. For example, if you do a lot with dramas, you will need someone to coordinate these with the OTC messages.
- Work with the OTC core team to develop the timeline and implementation plan.
- Oversee the ordering and distribution of OTC materials throughout the OTC experience.
- Oversee the OTC information center, making sure it is always well stocked with the needed materials as well as a knowledgeable volunteer who can answer questions.

Ministry Position Description for Small-Group Point Person

The small-group point person champions OTC at the small-group level. By recruiting, equipping, and supporting small-group leaders, the point person assures that every person who wants to be in an OTC small group gets connected and has the opportunity to be part of a transforming small-group learning experience.

Responsibilities

- Work with the OTC core team to lay out the implementation plan and timeline.
- Recruit and orient small-group leaders to lead OTC small groups.
- Communicate with the OTC congregational point person about materials needed for small groups.
- Communicate with the congregation (in partnership with the OTC core team) about the value of being in an OTC small group.
- Form small groups, making sure all those who want to participate can connect in a group.
- Give regular encouragement to small-group leaders throughout the OTC experience.

Ministry Position Description for Programming Point Person

The programming point person builds a team of volunteers who implement the OTC's unique programming elements. All programming elements needed to effectively run the OTC—video segments, PowerPoint® presentations, and so on—are included in the four OTC kits. The programming point person shapes these elements to customize them to the unique needs of your church and oversees the technical aspects of implementing them.

Responsibilities

- Work with the OTC core team to lay out the implementation plan and timeline.
- Recruit and prepare a team of people to support the OTC on a programming level. You will need a team to handle a variety of programming elements, including drama, props, PowerPoint®, video, cameras, and so on.
- Maintain consistent communication with the OTC champion (and teaching team) to be sure you are always prepared to give the program support needed for each OTC message.
- Give consistent encouragement to the programming team throughout the OTC experience.

PARTICIPANT COVENANT

BEFORE GOD AND IN COMMUNITY WITH GOD'S PEOPLE IN THIS CONGREGATION, I COMMIT TO:

- Pray faithfully for our OTC teacher(s).
- Attend weekly OTC services with an open heart to learn.
- Participate in an OTC small group.
- Follow one of the OTC weekly reading guides (circle one):

THIRTY-TWO-WEEK "FAST TRACK" READING GUIDE

FORTY-WEEK "COMPLETE TRACK" READING GUIDE

SIGNED: ______________________________ DATE: __________

Hundred-Question Biblical Literacy Test

1. How many spies did Moses send from Kadesh Barnea to spy out the Promised Land?
  a. 4
  b. 5
  c. 10
  d. 12

2. The Minor Prophets Nahum and Jonah both wrote books with a message to which city?
  a. Jerusalem
  b. Nineveh
  c. Samaria
  d. Babylon

3. In the third chapter of Genesis:
  a. Adam was deceived by a snake.
  b. There was a worldwide flood.
  c. Cain was born.
  d. The serpent deceived Eve.

4. The rise and fall of world empires is foretold in what Bible book?
  a. Ezekiel
  b. Zechariah
  c. Daniel
  d. Jeremiah

5. Nebuchadnezzar was king of:
  a. Egypt
  b. Babylon
  c. Persia
  d. Assyria

6. In the book of Joshua, Achan's sin caused Israel's defeat at what city?
  a. Ai
  b. Cairo
  c. Bethel
  d. Gaza

7. Boaz demonstrates the kinsman-redeemer principle in which book?
  a. Esther
  b. Job
  c. Ruth
  d. Isaiah

8. Who buried Moses?
  a. Aaron, his brother
  b. Miriam, his sister
  c. God, his God
  d. Joshua, his successor

9. Who was king of Babylon when Daniel interpreted the handwriting on the wall?
  a. Belshazzar
  b. Nebuchadnezzar
  c. Cyrus
  d. Elvis

10. Bethlehem, as the birthplace of Jesus, is talked about in which book?
  a. Micah
  b. Zechariah
  c. Zephaniah
  d. Isaiah

11. Moses' authority was challenged in the wilderness by whom?
  a. Aaron
  b. Dothan
  c. Korah
  d. Eleazar

12. Which of the following contains short wisdom sayings?
  a. Lamentations
  b. Proverbs
  c. Ecclesiastes
  d. Job

13. The Days of Purim are celebrated by the telling of the story found in which book?
  a. Ezra
  b. Habakkuk
  c. Esther
  d. Haggai

14. The reconstruction of the temple in Jerusalem is highlighted in which book?
  a. Hezekiah
  b. Haggai
  c. Esther
  d. Ezra

15. Jacob married how many of Laban's daughters?
  a. 2
  b. 3
  c. 4
  d. 1

16. "A little sleep, a little slumber, a little folding of the hands to rest" comes from which book?
  a. Psalms
  b. Proverbs
  c. Lamentations
  d. Song of Solomon

17. The historical event of Elijah calling fire down from God is in which book?
  a. Hezekiah
  b. Joshua
  c. 1 Kings
  d. Isaiah

18. King David was born in which city?
  a. Gaza
  b. Bethlehem
  c. Jericho
  d. Jerusalem

19. Who was the female judge?
a. Esther
b. Hannah
c. Abigail
d. Deborah

20. What animal being lost/let go in the wilderness each year demonstrated God's forgetting Israel's sins?
a. goat
b. horse
c. cow
d. deer

21. Who led the first group of Jews back to Israel from captivity?
a. Ezra
b. Nehemiah
c. Zerubbabel
d. Haggai

22. The naming of a place Babel and the mixing up of languages happened in which book?
a. Numbers
b. Deuteronomy
c. Genesis
d. Exodus

23. Though Ruth was from Moab, she would not stop following her mother-in-law, named:
a. Esther
b. Naomi
c. Hannah
d. Sarah

24. Who kept telling Job to "Curse God and die!"?
a. Bildad
b. Eliphaz
c. Zophar
d. Job's wife

25. Which event happened the latest in the Old Testament?
a. David crowned king
b. Elisha being called "you baldhead"
c. Jericho destroyed
d. Samson's haircut

26. "I know that my Redeemer lives" comes from which book?
a. Job
b. Psalms
c. Ecclesiastes
d. Proverbs

27. The story of a prophet getting put into a well is found in which book?
a. Ezekiel
b. Jeremiah
c. Isaiah
d. Daniel

28. Who was the woman who learned Samson's secret about his hair?
a. Delilah
b. Miriam
c. Jezebel
d. Jael

29. Who lived through Israel's wilderness experience and were the only ones of their generation to enter the Promised Land?
a. Saul/Jonathan
b. Shadrach/Meshach
c. Caleb/Joshua
d. David/Goliath

30. Under Gideon's leadership, how many men did God use to defeat the Midianites?
a. 35.000
b. 10,000
c. 1,000
d. 300

31. What plague did God bring on the Philistines for capturing Israel's ark of the covenant?
a. frogs and toads
b. boils and mice
c. flies and fleas
d. drought and famine

32. Who was the Israelite judge who anointed Saul as the first king of Israel?
a. Ehud
b. Gideon
c. Samuel
d. Eli

33. "Trust in the LORD with all your heart and lean not on your own understanding" is a quote from which book?
a. Job
b. Psalms
c. Proverbs
d. Isaiah

34. To whom did Mordecai say, "Who knows but that you have come to royal position for such a time as this"?
a. Esther
b. Jezebel
c. Ruth
d. Bathsheba

35. "Enter his gates with thanksgiving and his courts with praise" is from which book?
a. Isaiah
b. Job
c. Jeremiah
d. Psalms

36. The fifth book of the Bible is:
a. Exodus
b. Deuteronomy
c. Leviticus
d. Numbers

37. The life and times of Abraham are told in which book?
a. Numbers
b. Genesis
c. Exodus
d. Joshua

38. Who was Moses' brother and the first high priest of Israel?
a. Annas
b. Caiaphas
c. Eli
d. Aaron

39. Which book begins to tell the history of Israel as they enter the Promised Land?
a. Joshua
b. Judges
c. Deuteronomy
d. Numbers

40. What relationship was Moses to Jethro?
a. son
b. son-in-law
c. brother
d. father

41. Who is known as the "weeping prophet" because of his book of Lamentations?
a. Ezekiel
b. Daniel
c. Jeremiah
d. Job

42. Which book portrays the rightful place of physical love only within marriage?
a. Psalms
b. Micah
c. Song of Songs
d. Ruth

43. Which book contains the story of David the shepherd boy slaying the giant Goliath?
a. 1 Samuel
b. 2 Samuel
c. 1 Kings
d. Judges

44. When the Promised Land was being divided up, who asked for the hardest to conquer lands—the hill country of Hebron?
a. Joshua
b. Simon
c. Caleb
d. Levi

45. Whose name did God change to "Israel"?
a. Abraham
b. Isaac
c. Jacob
d. Joseph

46. Who said, "To obey is better than sacrifice, and to heed is better than the fat of rams"?
a. Samuel
b. Joshua
c. Nehemiah
d. David

47. The description of the destruction of the temple in Jerusalem by Babylon is in which book?
a. 2 Samuel
b. 2 Kings
c. 1 Chronicles
d. 1 Kings

48. Which Jewish exile was known as the "cupbearer to the king"?
a. Daniel
b. Shadrach
c. Ezra
d. Nehemiah

49. Before Joseph died, he made the sons of Israel swear an oath. It included which point?
a. burial next to Benjamin
b. build an altar honoring Jacob
c. carry his bones from Egypt
d. burial in Egypt

50. Who was the prophet who owned a donkey that saved his life and talked to him?
a. Ahab
b. Elisha
c. Balaam
d. Elijah

51. Who was the Moabite woman in the lineage of King David and was his great grandmother?
a. Naomi
b. Esther
c. Miriam
d. Ruth

52. Who was known as a "man after [God's] own heart"?
a. David
b. Jonathan
c. Solomon
d. Moses

53. Which of Israel's twelve tribes was given wholly to the Lord as his own in place of all of the firstborn sons in Israel?
a. Reuben
b. Levi
c. Judah
d. Dan

54. The book of Ruth takes place during which days?
a. when the judges ruled
b. after King Saul ruled
c. before Joshua conquered the land
d. during Solomon's time

55. Which statement did Job *not* say?
a. Man is born for trouble, as the sparks fly upward.
b. Woe is me. For I am a man of unclean lips.
c. Your hands shaped me and made me. Will you now turn and destroy me?
d. Though he slay me, I will hope in him.

56. In what country did the book of Esther take place?
a. Palestine
b. Egypt
c. Persia
d. Syria

57. The book of Judges contains this person's story.
a. Jonathan
b. Joshua
c. Samson
d. Saul

58. "Blessed is the man who does not walk in the counsel of the wicked" is taken from where?
a. Psalm 1
b. Psalm 23
c. Psalm 51
d. Psalm 100

59. What was Nehemiah's great work?
a. to be a king of Israel
b. to rebuild the walls of Jerusalem
c. to rebel against the Romans
d. to be a courageous priest

60. What book speaks of beginnings?
a. Genesis
b. Exodus
c. Leviticus
d. Deuteronomy

61. The book of Ecclesiastes was written by whom?
a. the Preacher
b. the son of David
c. the king in Jerusalem
d. all of the above

62. Which prophet related a vision of a valley of dry bones that live again?
a. Obadiah
b. Ezekiel
c. Amos
d. Nahum

63. The miracle in which the sun stood still is recorded in which book?
a. Leviticus
b. Joshua
c. Judges
d. 1 Samuel

64. The name Eve means:
a. Adam's helper
b. bone of my bones
c. mother of all living
d. created in the evening

65. Who hid two spies for Israel in Jericho?
a. Rachel
b. Ruth
c. Esther
d. Rahab

66. Who said, "Entreat me not to leave thee, or to return from following after thee" (from the King James Version)?
a. Ruth
b. Esther
c. Deborah
d. Orpah

67. "In the year that King Uzziah died," who saw a vision of God "high and exalted"?
a. Daniel
b. Ezekiel
c. Isaiah
d. Jeremiah

68. "The LORD said to Satan, 'Where have you come from?' Satan answered the LORD and said, 'From roaming through the earth and going back and forth in it,' " is from which book?
a. Ezekiel
b. Job
c. Isaiah
d. Jeremiah

69. Who received a hip injury while wrestling with an angel?
a. Isaac
b. Judah
c. David
d. Jacob

70. Which of the following was not one of Noah's three sons?
a. Shem
b. Ham
c. Jephthah
d. Japheth

71. Who was the man who "walked with God [and] ... God took him away," so that he did not physically die?
a. Jeremiah
b. Elisha
c. Job
d. Enoch

72. What do you remember about Jephthah from the book of Judges?
a. He made a rash vow and lived to regret it.
b. He was a Nazirite.
c. He fought the enemy with only a trumpet.
d. He was one of the sons of Noah.

73. From the book of Daniel we learn that the laws of the Medes and Persians:
a. affected only captives
b. could only be changed by the king
c. did not protect the life of the queen
d. could not be revoked by man

74. In which book does Cyrus, king of Persia, decree the rebuilding of the temple in Jerusalem?
a. Esther
b. Ezra
c. 1 Chronicles
d. Nehemiah

75. Which book details God telling Moses to strike a rock in order to get drinking water?
a. Exodus
b. Deuteronomy
c. Numbers
d. Joshua

76. Who said, "How long will you waver between two opinions? If the LORD is God, follow him; but if Baal is God, follow him"?
a. Elisha
b. Elijah
c. Joshua
d. Samuel

77. Who prayed that his servant's eyes would be open to see the armies of heaven surrounding them?
a. Ezekiel
b. Elijah
c. Elisha
d. Ehud

78. Which prophet was commanded by God to marry a prostitute as an object lesson to Israel?
a. Habakkuk
b. Hezekiah
c. Nahum
d. Hosea

79. Who was known as a hairy man compared to Jacob being smooth?
a. Abimelech
b. Judah
c. Esau
d. Isaac

80. What infamous king of Israel (of the northern ten tribes) disguised himself in battle but got hit by a randomly shot arrow and died?
a. Hezekiah
b. Ahab
c. Jeroboam
d. Rehoboam

81. Which judge of Israel was able to sneak a sword past the guards because he was left-handed?
a. Ehud
b. Gideon
c. Barak
d. Samuel

82. Which of these events happened the latest in the Old Testament?
a. Elijah flees to Horeb.
b. David conquers Jerusalem.
c. Josiah institutes a revival.
d. Elisha heals Namaan.

83. Namaan, whom Elisha healed of leprosy, was a military man from which country?
a. Israel
b. Aram
c. Egypt
d. Assyria

84. Samson was under what kind of vow?
a. chastity
b. Nazirite
c. silence
d. poverty

85. For what did Solomon pray to God?
a. wealth
b. wisdom
c. fame
d. humility

86. What swallowed Jonah?
a. a whale
b. Leviathan
c. a great fish
d. a great white shark

87. Which Minor Prophet identifies himself as a herdsman and grower of figs?
a. Joel
b. Jonah
c. Amos
d. Andy

88. "But the righteous will live by his faith," though quoted in Romans, was penned by which prophet?
a. Habakkuk
b. Joel
c. Amos
d. Jonah

89. Who was the postexilic prophet who encouraged the rebuilding of the temple?
a. Joel
b. Haggai
c. Amos
d. Obadiah

90. Which prophet was fed by ravens after announcing a drought?
a. Elisha
b. Isaiah
c. Jeremiah
d. Elijah

91. Which son did Jacob think he had lost to a wild animal?
a. Benjamin
b. Reuben
c. Joseph
d. Judah

92. The "Mizpah" benediction—"May the LORD watch between you and me when we are away from each other"—was given in which context?
a. love
b. distrust
c. wishing God's protection
d. blessing

93. Nathan the prophet confronted which man with his sin by telling a story about a sheep?
a. Solomon
b. Saul
c. Jonathan
d. David

94. Which son of David rebelled against his dad and declared himself king?
a. Solomon
b. Absalom
c. Amnon
d. Mephibosheth

95. Which event happened first?
a. King David's reign as king
b. the writing of Proverbs
c. Purim
d. Samuel in the tabernacle

96. "For to us a child is born, to us a son is given" is found in which Major Prophet's book?
a. Jeremiah
b. Isaiah
c. Ezekiel
d. Daniel

97. The last plague on Egypt took what from the Egyptians?
a. cows
b. pigs
c. sons
d. water

98. How many people were there on the ark during the Flood?
a. 8
b. 12
c. 6
d. 7

99. In which city was Abram, who became Abraham, living when he first followed God's leading?
a. Ur of the Chaldeans
b. Haran
c. Canaan
d. Jerusalem

100. Abraham had how many sons?
a. 8
b. 1
c. 3
d. 2
e. Many

Answers to the Hundred-Question Biblical Literacy Test

1. How many spies did Moses send from Kadesh Barnea to spy out the Promised Land?
a. 4
b. 5
c. 10
d. 12

2. The Minor Prophets Nahum and Jonah both wrote books with a message to which city?
a. Jerusalem
b. Nineveh
c. Samaria
d. Babylon

3. In the third chapter of Genesis:
a. Adam was deceived by a snake.
b. There was a worldwide flood.
c. Cain was born.
d. The serpent deceived Eve.

4. The rise and fall of world empires is foretold in what Bible book?
a. Ezekiel
b. Zechariah
c. Daniel
d. Jeremiah

5. Nebuchadnezzar was king of:
a. Egypt
b. Babylon
c. Persia
d. Assyria

6. In the book of Joshua, Achan's sin caused Israel's defeat at what city?
a. Ai
b. Cairo
c. Bethel
d. Gaza

7. Boaz demonstrates the kinsman-redeemer principle in which book?
a. Esther
b. Job
c. Ruth
d. Isaiah

8. Who buried Moses?
a. Aaron, his brother
b. Miriam, his sister
c. God, his God
d. Joshua, his successor

9. Who was king of Babylon when Daniel interpreted the handwriting on the wall?
a. Belshazzar
b. Nebuchadnezzar
c. Cyrus
d. Elvis

10. Bethlehem, as the birthplace of Jesus, is talked about in which book?
a. Micah
b. Zechariah
c. Zephaniah
d. Isaiah

11. Moses' authority was challenged in the wilderness by whom?
a. Aaron
b. Dothan
c. Korah
d. Eleazar

12. Which of the following contains short wisdom sayings?
a. Lamentations
b. Proverbs
c. Ecclesiastes
d. Job

13. The Days of Purim are celebrated by the telling of the story found in which book?
a. Ezra
b. Habakkuk
c. Esther
d. Haggai

14. The reconstruction of the temple in Jerusalem is highlighted in which book?
a. Hezekiah
b. Haggai
c. Esther
d. Ezra

15. Jacob married how many of Laban's daughters?
a. 2
b. 3
c. 4
d. 1

16. "A little sleep, a little slumber, a little folding of the hands to rest" comes from which book?
a. Psalms
b. Proverbs
c. Lamentations
d. Song of Solomon

17. The historical event of Elijah calling fire down from God is in which book?
a. Hezekiah
b. Joshua
c. 1 Kings
d. Isaiah

18. King David was born in which city?
a. Gaza
b. Bethlehem
c. Jericho
d. Jerusalem

19. Who was the female judge?
a. Esther
b. Hannah
c. Abigail
d. Deborah

20. What animal being lost/let go in the wilderness each year demonstrated God's forgetting Israel's sins?
a. goat
b. horse
c. cow
d. deer

21. Who led the first group of Jews back to Israel from captivity?
a. Ezra
b. Nehemiah
c. Zerubbabel
d. Haggai

22. The naming of a place Babel and the mixing up of languages happened in which book?
a. Numbers
b. Deuteronomy
c. Genesis
d. Exodus

23. Though Ruth was from Moab, she would not stop following her mother-in-law, named:
a. Esther
b. Naomi
c. Hannah
d. Sarah

24. Who kept telling Job to "Curse God and die!"?
a. Bildad
b. Eliphaz
c. Zophar
d. Job's wife

25. Which event happened the latest in the Old Testament?
- a. David crowned king
- **b. Elisha being called "you baldhead"**
- c. Jericho destroyed
- d. Samson's haircut

26. "I know that my Redeemer lives" comes from which book?
- **a. Job**
- b. Psalms
- c. Ecclesiastes
- d. Proverbs

27. The story of a prophet getting put into a well is found in which book?
- a. Ezekiel
- **b. Jeremiah**
- c. Isaiah
- d. Daniel

28. Who was the woman who learned Samson's secret about his hair?
- **a. Delilah**
- b. Miriam
- c. Jezebel
- d. Jael

29. Who lived through Israel's wilderness experience and were the only ones of their generation to enter the Promised Land?
- a. Saul/Jonathan
- b. Shadrach/Meshach
- **c. Caleb/Joshua**
- d. David/Goliath

30. Under Gideon's leadership, how many men did God use to defeat the Midianites?
- a. 35.000
- b. 10,000
- c. 1,000
- **d. 300**

31. What plague did God bring on the Philistines for capturing Israel's ark of the covenant?
- a. frogs and toads
- **b. boils and mice**
- c. flies and fleas
- d. drought and famine

32. Who was the Israelite judge who anointed Saul as the first king of Israel?
- a. Ehud
- b. Gideon
- **c. Samuel**
- d. Eli

33. "Trust in the LORD with all your heart and lean not on your own understanding" is a quote from which book?
- a. Job
- b. Psalms
- **c. Proverbs**
- d. Isaiah

34. To whom did Mordecai say, "Who knows but that you have come to royal position for such a time as this"?
- **a. Esther**
- b. Jezebel
- c. Ruth
- d. Bathsheba

35. "Enter his gates with thanksgiving and his courts with praise" is from which book?
- a. Isaiah
- b. Job
- c. Jeremiah
- **d. Psalms**

36. The fifth book of the Bible is:
- a. Exodus
- **b. Deuteronomy**
- c. Leviticus
- d. Numbers

37. The life and times of Abraham are told in which book?
- a. Numbers
- **b. Genesis**
- c. Exodus
- d. Joshua

38. Who was Moses' brother and the first high priest of Israel?
- a. Annas
- b. Caiaphas
- c. Eli
- **d. Aaron**

39. Which book begins to tell the history of Israel as they enter the Promised Land?
- **a. Joshua**
- b. Judges
- c. Deuteronomy
- d. Numbers

40. What relationship was Moses to Jethro?
- a. son
- **b. son-in-law**
- c. brother
- d. father

41. Who is known as the "weeping prophet" because of his book of Lamentations?
- a. Ezekiel
- b. Daniel
- **c. Jeremiah**
- d. Job

42. Which book portrays the rightful place of physical love only within marriage?
- a. Psalms
- b. Micah
- **c. Song of Songs**
- d. Ruth

43. Which book contains the story of David the shepherd boy slaying the giant Goliath?
- **a. 1 Samuel**
- b. 2 Samuel
- c. 1 Kings
- d. Judges

44. When the Promised Land was being divided up, who asked for the hardest to conquer lands —the hill country of Hebron?
- a. Joshua
- b. Simon
- **c. Caleb**
- d. Levi

45. Whose name did God change to "Israel"?
- a. Abraham
- b. Isaac
- **c. Jacob**
- d. Joseph

46. Who said, "To obey is better than sacrifice, and to heed is better than the fat of rams"?
- **a. Samuel**
- b. Joshua
- c. Nehemiah
- d. David

47. The description of the destruction of the temple in Jerusalem by Babylon is in which book?
- a. 2 Samuel
- **b. 2 Kings**
- c. 1 Chronicles
- d. 1 Kings

48. Which Jewish exile was known as the "cupbearer to the king"?
- a. Daniel
- b. Shadrach
- c. Ezra
- **d. Nehemiah**

49. Before Joseph died, he made the sons of Israel swear an oath. It included which point?
- a. burial next to Benjamin
- b. build an altar honoring Jacob
- **c. carry his bones from Egypt**
- d. burial in Egypt

50. Who was the prophet who owned a donkey that saved his life and talked to him?
- a. Ahab
- b. Elisha
- **c. Balaam**
- d. Elijah

51. Who was the Moabite woman in the lineage of King David and was his great grandmother?
- a. Naomi
- b. Esther
- c. Miriam
- **d. Ruth**

52. Who was known as a "man after [God's] own heart"?
- **a. David**
- b. Jonathan
- c. Solomon
- d. Moses

53. Which of Israel's twelve tribes was given wholly to the Lord as his own in place of all of the firstborn sons in Israel?
- a. Reuben
- **b. Levi**
- c. Judah
- d. Dan

54. The book of Ruth takes place during which days?
- **a. when the judges ruled**
- b. after King Saul ruled
- c. before Joshua conquered the land
- d. during Solomon's time

55. Which statement did Job *not* say?
- a. Man is born for trouble, as the sparks fly upward
- **b. Woe is me. For I am a man of unclean lips.**
- c. Your hands shaped me and made me. Will you now turn and destroy me?
- d. Though he slay me, I will hope in him.

56. In what country did the book of Esther take place?
- a. Palestine
- b. Egypt
- **c. Persia**
- d. Syria

57. The book of Judges contains this person's story.
- a. Jonathan
- b. Joshua
- **c. Samson**
- d. Saul

58. "Blessed is the man who does not walk in the counsel of the wicked" is taken from where?
- **a. Psalm 1**
- b. Psalm 23
- c. Psalm 51
- d. Psalm 100

59. What was Nehemiah's great work?
- a. to be a king of Israel
- **b. to rebuild the walls of Jerusalem**
- c. to rebel against the Romans
- d. to be a courageous priest

60. What book speaks of beginnings?
- **a. Genesis**
- b. Exodus
- c. Leviticus
- d. Deuteronomy

61. The book of Ecclesiastes was written by whom?
- a. the Preacher
- b. the son of David
- c. the king in Jerusalem
- **d. all of the above**

62. Which prophet related a vision of a valley of dry bones that live again?
- a. Obadiah
- **b. Ezekiel**
- c. Amos
- d. Nahum

63. The miracle in which the sun stood still is recorded in which book?
- a. Leviticus
- **b. Joshua**
- c. Judges
- d. 1 Samuel

64. The name Eve means:
- a. Adam's helper
- b. bone of my bones
- **c. mother of all living**
- d. created in the evening

65. Who hid two spies for Israel in Jericho?
- a. Rachel
- b. Ruth
- c. Esther
- **d. Rahab**

66. Who said, "Entreat me not to leave thee, or to return from following after thee" (from the King James Version)?
- **a. Ruth**
- b. Esther
- c. Deborah
- d. Orpah

67. "In the year that King Uzziah died," who saw a vision of God "high and exalted"?
- a. Daniel
- b. Ezekiel
- **c. Isaiah**
- d. Jeremiah

68. "The LORD said to Satan, 'Where have you come from?' Satan answered the LORD and said, 'From roaming through the earth and going back and forth in it,' " is from which book?
- a. Ezekiel
- **b. Job**
- c. Isaiah
- d. Jeremiah

69. Who received a hip injury while wrestling with an angel?
- a. Isaac
- b. Judah
- c. David
- **d. Jacob**

70. Which of the following was not one of Noah's three sons?
- a. Shem
- b. Ham
- **c. Jephthah**
- d. Japheth

71. Who was the man who "walked with God [and] ... God took him away," so that he did not physically die?
- a. Jeremiah
- b. Elisha
- c. Job
- **d. Enoch**

72. What do you remember about Jephthah from the book of Judges?
- **a. He made a rash vow and lived to regret it.**
- b. He was a Nazirite.
- c. He fought the enemy with only a trumpet.
- d. He was one of the sons of Noah.

73. From the book of Daniel we learn that the laws of the Medes and Persians:
- a. affected only captives
- b. could only be changed by the king
- c. did not protect the life of the queen
- **d. could not be revoked by man**

74. In which book does Cyrus, king of Persia, decree the rebuilding of the temple in Jerusalem?
- a. Esther
- **b. Ezra**
- c. 1 Chronicles
- d. Nehemiah

75. Which book details the story of God telling Moses to strike a rock in order to get drinking water?
- **a. Exodus**
- b. Deuteronomy
- c. Numbers
- d. Joshua

76. Who said, "How long will you waver between two opinions? If the LORD is God, follow him; but if Baal is God, follow him"?
- a. Elisha
- **b. Elijah**
- c. Joshua
- d. Samuel

77. Who prayed that his servant's eyes would be open to see the armies of heaven surrounding them?
- a. Ezekiel
- b. Elijah
- **c. Elisha**
- d. Ehud

78. Which prophet was commanded by God to marry a prostitute as an object lesson to Israel?
- a. Habakkuk
- b. Hezekiah
- c. Nahum
- **d. Hosea**

79. Who was known as a hairy man compared to Jacob being smooth?
- a. Abimelech
- b. Judah
- **c. Esau**
- d. Isaac

80. What infamous king of Israel (of the northern ten tribes) disguised himself in battle but got hit by a randomly shot arrow and died?
a. Hezekiah
b. Ahab
c. Jeroboam
d. Rehoboam

81. Which judge of Israel was able to sneak a sword past the guards because he was left-handed?
a. Ehud
b. Gideon
c. Barak
d. Samuel

82. Which of these events happened the latest in the Old Testament?
a. Elijah flees to Horeb.
b. David conquers Jerusalem.
c. Josiah institutes a revival.
d. Elisha heals Namaan.

83. Namaan, whom Elisha healed of leprosy, was a military man from which country?
a. Israel
b. Aram
c. Egypt
d. Assyria

84. Samson was under what kind of vow?
a. chastity
b. Nazirite
c. silence
d. poverty

85. For what did Solomon pray to God?
a. wealth
b. wisdom
c. fame
d. humility

86. What swallowed Jonah?
a. a whale
b. Leviathan
c. a great fish
d. a great white shark

87. Which Minor Prophet identifies himself as a herdsman and grower of figs?
a. Joel
b. Jonah
c. Amos
d. Andy

88. "But the righteous will live by his faith," though quoted in Romans, was penned by which prophet?
a. Habakkuk
b. Joel
c. Amos
d. Jonah

89. Who was the postexilic prophet who encouraged the rebuilding of the temple?
a. Joel
b. Haggai
c. Amos
d. Obadiah

90. Which prophet was fed by ravens after announcing a drought?
a. Elisha
b. Isaiah
c. Jeremiah
d. Elijah

91. Which son did Jacob think he had lost to a wild animal?
a. Benjamin
b. Reuben
c. Joseph
d. Judah

92. The "Mizpah" benediction—"May the LORD watch between you and me when we are away from each other"—was given in which context?
a. love
b. distrust
c. wishing God's protection
d. blessing

93. Nathan the prophet confronted which man with his sin by telling a story about a sheep?
a. Solomon
b. Saul
c. Jonathan
d. **David**

94. Which son of David rebelled against his dad and declared himself king?
a. Solomon
b. Absalom
c. Amnon
d. Mephibosheth

95. Which event happened first?
a. King David's reign as king
b. the writing of Proverbs
c. Purim
d. Samuel in the tabernacle

96. "For to us a child is born, to us a son is given" is found in which Major Prophet's book?
a. Jeremiah
b. Isaiah
c. Ezekiel
d. Daniel

97. The last plague on Egypt took what from the Egyptians?
a. cows
b. pigs
c. sons
d. water

98. How many people were there on the ark during the Flood?
a. 8
b. 12
c. 6
d. 7

99. In which city was Abram, who became Abraham, living when he first followed God's leading?
a. Ur of the Chaldeans
b. Haran
c. Canaan
d. Jerusalem

100. Abraham had how many sons?
a. 8
b. 1
c. 3
d. 2
e. Many

Willow Creek Association

Vision, Training, Resources for Prevailing Churches

This resource was created to serve you and to help you in building a local church that prevails!

Since 1992, the Willow Creek Association (WCA) has been linking like-minded, action-oriented churches with each other and with strategic vision, training, and resources. Now a worldwide network of over 6,400 churches from more than ninety denominations, the WCA works to equip Member Churches and others with the tools needed to build prevailing churches. Our desire is to inspire, equip, and encourage Christian leaders to build biblically functioning churches that reach increasing numbers of unchurched people, not just with innovations from Willow Creek Community Church in South Barrington, Illinois, but from any church in the world that has experienced God-given breakthroughs.

Willow Creek Conferences

Each year, thousands of local church leaders, staff and volunteers—from WCA Member Churches and others—attend one of our conferences or training events. Conferences offered on the Willow Creek campus in South Barrington, Illinois, include:

Prevailing Church Conference: Foundational training for staff and volunteers working to build a prevailing local church.

Prevailing Church Workshops: More than fifty strategic, day-long workshops covering seven topic areas that represent key characteristics of a prevailing church; offered twice each year.

Promiseland Conference: Children's ministries; infant through fifth grade.

Student Ministries Conference: Junior and senior high ministries.

Willow Creek Arts Conference: Vision and training for Christian artists using their gifts in the ministries of local churches.

Leadership Summit: Envisioning and equipping Christians with leadership gifts and responsibilities; broadcast live via satellite to eighteen cities across North America.

Contagious Evangelism Conference: Encouragement and training for churches and church leaders who want to be strategic in reaching lost people for Christ.

Small Groups Conference: Exploring how developing a church *of* small groups can play a vital role in developing authentic Christian community that leads to spiritual transformation.

To find out more about WCA conferences, visit our website at www.willowcreek.com.

Prevailing Church Regional Workshops

Each year the WCA team leads several, two-day training events in select cities across the United States. Some twenty day-long workshops are offered in topic areas including leadership, next-generation ministries, small groups, arts and worship, evangelism, spiritual gifts, financial stewardship, and spiritual formation. These events make quality training more accessible and affordable to larger groups of staff and volunteers.

To find out more about Prevailing Church Regional Workshops, visit our website at www.willowcreek.com.

Willow Creek Resources™

Churches can look to Willow Creek Resources™ for a trusted channel of ministry tools in areas of leadership, evangelism, spiritual gifts, small groups, drama, contemporary music, financial stewardship, spiritual transformation, and more. For ordering information, call (800) 570-9812 or visit our website at www.willowcreek.com.

WCA Membership

Membership in the Willow Creek Association as well as attendance at WCA Conferences is for churches, ministries, and leaders who hold to a historic, orthodox understanding of biblical Christianity. The annual church membership fee of $249 provides substantial discounts for your entire team on all conferences and Willow Creek Resources, networking opportunities with other outreach-oriented churches, a bimonthly newsletter, a subscription to the *Defining Moments* monthly audio journal for leaders, and more.

To find out more about WCA membership, visit our website at www.willowcreek.com.

WillowNet (www.willowcreek.com)

This Internet resource service provides access to hundreds of Willow Creek messages, drama scripts, songs, videos, and multimedia ideas. The system allows you to sort through these elements and download them for a fee.

Our website also provides detailed information on the Willow Creek Association, Willow Creek Community Church, WCA membership, conferences, training events, resources, and more.

WillowCharts.com (www.willowcharts.com)

Designed for local church worship leaders and musicians, WillowCharts.com provides online access to hundreds of music charts and chart components, including choir, orchestral, and horn sections, as well as rehearsal tracks and video streaming of Willow Creek Community Church performances.

The NET (http://studentministry.willowcreek.com)

The NET is an online training and resource center designed by and for student ministry leaders. It provides an inside look at the structure, vision, and mission of prevailing student ministries from around the world. The NET gives leaders access to complete programming elements, including message outlines, dramas, small group questions, and more. An indispensable resource and networking tool for prevailing student ministry leaders!

Contact the Willow Creek Association

If you have comments or questions, or would like to find out more about WCA events or resources, please contact us:

Willow Creek Association
P.O. Box 3188, Barrington, IL 60011-3188
Phone: (800) 570-9812 or (847) 765-0070
Fax (888) 922-0035 or (847) 765-5046
Web: www.willowcreek.com